Editor
Eric Migliaccio

Managing Editor
Ina Massler Levin, M.A.

Editor-in-Chief
Sharon Coan, M.S. Ed.

Illustrator
Howard Chaney

Cover Artist
Denice Adorno

Art Coordinator
Denice Adorno

Imaging
James Edward Grace
Rosa C. See

Product Manager
Phil Garcia

Publishers
Rachelle Cracchiolo, M.S. Ed.
Mary Dupuy Smith, M.S. Ed.

Developing LISTENING SKILLS

Author

Debra J. Housel, M.S. Ed.

Teacher Created Materials

Teacher Created Materials, Inc.
6421 Industry Way
Westminster, CA 92683
www.teachercreated.com
ISBN-1-57690-65
©2001 Teacher Created M
Made in U.S.A

D1406944

Table of Contents

Introduction 3

How to Use This Book 4

Basic Listening Skill-Building Activities 7

Differentiating Between Fact & Opinion 15

Key Words that Signal Important Information 17

Folktales 18

    Outline Student Guide—Graphic Organizer—Folktales—Answer Key

Literature Selections 47

    Outline Student Guide—Graphic Organizer—Literature Selections—Answer Key

Magazine Articles 68

  Magazine Articles About Non-Living Things

    Outline Student Guide—Graphic Organizer—Articles about Non-Living Things—
    Answer Key

  Magazine Articles About Living Things

    Outline Student Guide —Graphic Organizer—Articles about Living Things—Answer Key

  Famous Persons

    Outline Student Guide—Graphic Organizer—Famous Persons—Answer Key

Newspaper Articles 128

  Newspaper Articles About Places

    Outline Student Guide—Graphic Organizer—Articles about Places—Answer Key

  Newspaper Articles About Events

    Outline Student Guide—Graphic Organizer—Articles about Events—Answer Key

Bibliography 160

Introduction

Instruction in listening is as crucial as instruction in reading and writing. Listening permeates every facet of school curriculum, and the academic environment itself demands that children possess competent listening skills in order to learn. Active listening is necessary for following directions, understanding concepts, maintaining discipline, and planning classroom activities. Effective listening skills correlate closely with such essential reading behaviors as auditory memory and reading with expression. In addition, research has proven that acquiring better listening skills (auditory comprehension) yields substantial benefits in the area of reading comprehension. Consequently, we all want our students to become better listeners, to understand and remember information they hear, and to take adequate notes when necessary. However, accomplishing this feat often seems difficult, even elusive. *Developing Listening Skills* offers a logical, sequential, step-by-step process to help third through fifth grade students recognize what information is important, take effective notes, and demonstrate their understanding through written responses.

Listening for Information

Every day we hear all sorts of information without seeing it written anywhere—loudspeaker announcements, radio ads, and weather forecasts are a few examples. We need to attend to these messages and sometimes act on them. In school, listening takes on additional importance because a great deal of learning involves taking appropriate notes for later study and review. Knowing what's been said gives the student greater confidence to ask questions without the fear of looking foolish ("He just answered that about two minutes ago."). In addition, the ability to take notes while listening is critical for success in high school and college, so the development of these skills needs to begin early in a child's educational career. Writing information down reinforces what a student hears and helps him or her remember it. Taking notes promotes active listening, and educational studies have shown that the cognitive processes associated with hearing, comprehending, and writing provide the best reinforcement of material. The student guide pages given in this book will help your students establish notetaking skills using a variety of methods (informal outlines, semantic mapping, graphic organizers), each suited to a specific purpose. After using the guide pages about four times, the children should have an idea of the specific data they're looking for when listening for information.

Listening Level

A person's listening level is the level at which he or she can comprehend material that is read to him or her. Since research has established that a child's listening level is approximately two years beyond his or her reading level, the passages presented in *Developing Listening Skills* are written at reading levels that span fourth through seventh grades.

Building Listening Ability

To ensure that students possess the requisite skills to succeed with the passages, this book contains preliminary listening-building activities. These activities should take place prior to beginning the actual listening passages and essay responses. Also, research has shown that short, intensive listening periods work best, as kids tune out when they must listen intently for too long.

Promote Student Success

Before beginning any genre, discuss the important characteristics of that genre. For example, before doing the first folktale, discuss with the students what a moral is and how a fable teaches a moral through implication rather than a direct statement. You may want to use a folktale from another source to demonstrate this point. Prior to the literature passages, talk to your students about the elements of literature: characters, setting, theme, main conflict/crisis, resolution, and the resolution's effect on characters. You can use a literary work the students are currently reading to illustrate these elements. Before beginning any of the nonfiction passages (magazine articles, newspaper articles, and famous person essays), ask your students questions such as, "What types of information are found in nonfiction? Why do people read nonfiction? How are fiction and nonfiction alike?" Engaging in these simple but necessary preparatory activities will greatly improve your students' ability to master the passages.

How to Use This Book

The first third of each genre (4 passages) is for instructional practice; the final two-thirds of each genre (8 passages) is for assessment practice. If necessary, you can modify this ratio to meet your students' needs.

Begin with the listening-building activities at the start of the book. When you feel the students have mastered the requisite skills, proceed to the passages. Since they build in difficulty, present the passages for each genre in the order given. Follow the administration directions closely, for they move from supported instructional practice to actual test-like practice.

You may wish to tape record the majority of passages so that you can play them for your class. In this way, you will only have to read the passages once, and yet you will be able to use them time and again over the years. However, you should not do this for the first and third passages in each genre, as these will need to be actively modeled by you. For those that you do record, be sure to speak loudly, clearly, and slowly into the tape recorder to avoid voice distortion.

Although the genres are presented in the order deemed logical by the author, it is not essential that you do one particular genre prior to another.

Note: After you complete the first few passages of one genre, you may want to do the first few of another genre, and so on, until you have covered the first few passages in each genre. Then use a rotation to complete the remaining passages of each genre. This staggering will encourage the students to think critically in order to decide the type of notes to take for a particular passage.

Passage #1

Carefully model the first passage in a genre as a whole-group lesson.

1. Choose the genre you'd like to begin with.

2. Copy and hand out to students the outline guide page for that genre. Read aloud the questions on the guide page and discuss them. Expand on the questions given by offering examples of different ways the answers may be phrased. For example, in response to the question "When?" the answer may be as vague as "about 250 years ago" or as precise as "June 23, 1958," depending on the passage. Advise the students to be ready to record either type of answer. Also be sure to explain that not all questions on the guide page will always be answered by the article.

3. Read the first passage through slowly, asking the students to just listen carefully the first time through. Tell them that you will read it again, and that's when they'll fill in the guide page.

4. Reread the passage. Do a "think aloud" to show students your own thought processes when tackling this task by stopping and saying, "I think this is important. Is it one of my questions? Yes! OK, I'll jot it down." Have them complete their guide page. At no time are they allowed to see the passage.

5. On an overhead projector, display the essay questions. Ask the students to refer to their guide page notes to tell you the answers to each essay question. Whenever they hesitate, do a "think aloud" as you complete the page in front of the class. Model suitable essay responses, making certain to mention the necessity for capitals and periods where appropriate.

How to Use This Book (cont.)

Passage #2

Give the students a bit more independence on the second passage.

1. Choose the second passage in the same genre.

2. Copy and hand out to the students the outline guide page for the genre. Review the questions on the guide page.

3. Read the passage slowly, allowing the students to write the answers to the questions on their guide pages.

4. Reread the passage and have them complete their guide page. At no time are they allowed to see the passage.

5. Hand them the essay questions. Tell them to refer to their notes from their guide page to generate their written responses.

6. Collect and score the essays.

7. On an overhead projector, display the essay questions. Read aloud an exemplary, average, and minimum essay response for each question (*without* revealing who the authors are!). Talk about what made them exemplary, average, and minimally acceptable. Discuss what would be unacceptable responses as well.

Passage #3

Carefully model the third passage of a genre as a whole-group lesson.

1. Copy and hand out to the students the graphic organizer guide page for the genre. Discuss with the class the purpose of the words, lines, and boxes on the graphic organizer. Give examples of different ways the information may be stated. For example, in response to the question "Where?" the answer may be as vague as "in the Indian Ocean" or as specific as "New York City," depending on the passage. Advise the students to be ready to record either type of answer. Also be sure to explain that the graphic organizer may not be completely filled up by the information given in an article.

2. Read the first passage through slowly, asking the students to just listen *carefully* the first time through. Tell them that you will read it again, and that's when they'll fill in the guide page.

3. Reread the passage. Do a "think aloud" to show students your own thought processes when tackling this task by stopping and saying, "I think this is important—is there a place to record it on my graphic organizer? Yes! OK, I'll write. . . ." Have them complete their graphic organizer guide page along with you. At no time are they allowed to see the passage.

4. Next, display the essay questions on an overhead projector. Ask the students to refer to their graphic organizers to tell you the answers to each essay question. Whenever they hesitate, do a "think aloud" as you complete the page in front of the class. Model suitable essay responses, making certain to mention the necessity for capitals and periods where appropriate.

How to Use This Book *(cont.)*

Passage #4

1. For the fourth passage in each genre, copy and hand out to the students the graphic organizer page. Remind them of the purpose of the words, lines, and boxes on the graphic organizer.

2. Read the passage slowly, allowing the students to write the answers to the questions on their guide pages. Then reread the passage and have them complete their guide page. At no time are they allowed to see the passage.

3. Hand them the essay questions. Tell them to refer to their notes from their graphic organizer page to generate their written responses.

4. Collect and score the essays.

5. On an overhead projector, display the essay questions. Read aloud an exemplary, average, and minimum essay response for each question (*without* revealing who the authors are). Talk about what made them exemplary, average, and minimally acceptable. Discuss what would be unacceptable responses as well.

Passages #5–12

Once you have covered the first four passages of each genre, move to the test-taking portion (the last eight passages of each genre, done without giving the students the appropriate guide pages). Encourage the students to follow the format of their favorite guide page while taking notes.

1. Slowly, but with expression, read aloud each passage to the students. Tell them just to listen *carefully* the first time through. Tell them you will read it again.

2. They should take notes on important details the second time. Remind them to think of what was included on the student guide pages. Read the passage aloud to the students a second time, slowly but with expression.

3. When you are done, pass out the essay questions. The students may use only the notes they have taken to answer the questions; *they may not see the passage at any time.* Also, they must not know the questions prior to listening to the passage twice. The notes are not considered part of the grade and are just for their own use.

4. Collect and score the essays.

5. On an overhead projector, display the essay questions. Read aloud an exemplary, average, and minimum essay response for each question (*without* revealing who the authors are). Talk about what made them exemplary, average, and minimally acceptable. Discuss what would be unacceptable responses as well.

Scoring Student Responses

To make scoring the essays as quick and easy as possible, adhere to the answer key's specific point value for each statement a student makes. If the statement is invalid or irrelevant, do not add or subtract anything. Total the points to arrive at an overall score, then refer to the rubrics given on the answer key pages for each genre to arrive at the minimum passing, average, and exemplary scores.

Basic Listening Skill-Building Activities

To develop students' basic listening skills and ensure success with the passages in this book, have your students complete some or all of the following exercises. The activities outlined here do not need to be done in any specific order nor are they all essential for every class. Use your judgment to select the ones that will provide the greatest benefit to your students.

Directed Listening

Objective: To develop the strategies of making predictions and monitoring one's own comprehension when listening

You can do this whenever you read a biographical or fictional book aloud to your class. Using the title, have the students predict what the story might be about. Read aloud to a good stopping point. Model a question about what has happened so far in the text. Then do a "think aloud" where you model your own metacognitive processes by summarizing what's been read so far and making a prediction such as, "I bet that . . . will happen next." Ask the students if they agree with your prediction. If they don't, have them state their own predictions. Read to the next good stopping point in the story. This time ask the students, "What do you think the author meant when he said . . . ? What makes you think so? Can you give an example?" Ask the students what they believe will happen next. Read to the end of the story. Discuss the story as a whole, being certain to talk about the predictions that were made and how the story would have been different if those predictions had come true.

Retelling

Objective: To increase attentiveness to characters, plot, and details

This exercise has the students demonstrate their listening skills by retelling a story that's been read to them. Tell them in advance that you will expect them to be able to retell the story, including details. One way to accomplish this objective is to read a story aloud to the whole class, then have each student individually state his or her name and then retell the story to a tape recorder. This enables you to review it at a time that's convenient for you without taking your attention away from the class. Another interesting way to do this is read a story to one child and ask that child to retell it to another.

Solve the Mystery

Objective: To enhance active listening and promote visualization of information received aurally

Read the children some of the descriptions on page 9. Have the students write the name of the mystery item and draw a picture of it. Depending on the age and ability of your students, you may at first need to read these descriptions twice to ensure students' success; move to a singular reading as soon as possible, though, as this will promote more attentive listening. Allow divergent answers if they make sense. Do two each day until the students demonstrate competence.

Complete the Sentence

Objective: To encourage students to anticipate a speaker's next point and to strengthen the ability to think while listening

Children (indeed, everyone) listen best when trying to predict what the speaker will say next. With small groups or the whole class, read a sentence, omitting an essential word by substituting "Hmmm" in its place. Then ask the child to write the word or phrase that could finish the sentence. Accept any answers that make sense. At first, you may need to read these descriptions twice to ensure students' success, but move to a singular reading as soon as possible. Do about five each day until students demonstrate competence. You can make up your own or use those on page 10.

Basic Listening Skill-Building Activities *(cont.)*

Finish the Story

Objectives: To reinforce the necessity of using context to predict while listening, to reinforce the fact that what they hear should make sense; to use their imaginations to respond to information received aurally

After students have achieved success with the complete-the-sentence exercises, they are ready for the new challenge of finishing a story. To use time wisely, limit the students to five sentences. Make up your own scenarios or use those on page 11. Do one each day until the students demonstrate competence.

Nonsense Sentences

Objective: To improve critical listening ability by reinforcing the fact that what they hear should make sense

Studies show that people listen better when trying to incorporate information heard with existing background knowledge (schema). Read aloud a sentence in which there is one word that renders the sentence void of meaning or creates a fantasy. Then ask a volunteer to identify what's wrong with the sentence and how it could be changed to make sense. There may be more than one way to modify the sentence to make it sensible. Make up your own nonsense sentences or use the ones on page 12. Do about five each day until the students demonstrate competence.

Which Word Doesn't Belong?

Objective: To improve the ability to listen critically to categorize information

With the entire class or small groups, read a list of four or five words (more than that is too complex for elementary-age children). Ask them to determine the word that doesn't belong to the group and write it on a piece of paper. Do about five of these following the same procedure. Then go back and reread the first group and ask which word they chose. Repeat with the second group. Make the students explain their answers, whether right or wrong, to clarify for those who are having difficulty. Create your own lists or use those on page 13. Do about five each day until the students demonstrate competence.

Listen, Then Do

Objective: To expand short-term memory and increase the ability to act on what's been heard

Tell the children that you will describe a task and then call on a child to do it. This will make the children listen carefully, since they don't know who will be asked to do it. Begin with one-step commands; once those are mastered, move to two-step and eventually three-step commands. Create your own tasks or use those on page 14. Do one each with three students daily until you've practiced a one-step, two-step, and three-step command with every child in your class.

Solve the Mystery

1. I am cold, but I can melt. I fall in winter. Usually kids like me better than adults. What am I? Draw a picture of me. (*snow*)

2. Some people have me in their backyards. I can be deep or shallow. People use me to cool off during the summer. What am I? Draw a picture of me. (*a pool*)

3. I smell like diesel fumes, and my motor rumbles. I have lots of seats and a driver. People ride on me to get where they need to go. What am I? Draw a picture of me. (*a bus*)

4. I am actually a very soft rock. I can come in many colors but yellow and white are the most common. Teachers use me to write on the board. What am I? Draw a picture of me. (*chalk*)

5. I'm usually rectangular. I can be thick or thin. Children look at my pictures and read my words. What am I? Draw a picture of me. (*a book*)

6. I pop up big and fold down small. I come in many colors. I'm handy to have during a rainstorm. What am I? Draw a picture of me. (*an umbrella*)

7. I fly in the sky, but I do not carry people. I hunt at night. When I see something to eat, I swoop down and grab it. What am I? Draw a picture of me. (*an owl;* a hawk or eagle hunts by day)

8. I am made of concrete. People walk on me every day. I keep them safe from walking in the street. What am I? Draw a picture of me. (*a sidewalk*)

9. You can see me almost anywhere. Children play games on me. I have a screen and a keyboard. What am I? Draw a picture of me. (*a computer*)

10. I am yellow and long. I grow in bunches in South America. Many people enjoy eating me. What am I? Draw a picture of me. (*bananas*)

11. People are very afraid of me. My strong, swirling winds destroy everything in my path. I happen mostly in Midwestern America. What am I? Draw a picture of me. (*a tornado;* hurricanes occur only on the East coast)

12. I am very useful. I can be digital or analog, plain or fancy. Sometimes I have hands. People glance at me to see if they are late. What am I? Draw a picture of me. (*a clock or watch*)

13. I am white and have many tiny grains, like sand. I can be found in a bag at the grocery store. I make things taste sweet. What am I? Draw a picture of me. (*sugar*)

14. I come in every color you can imagine. Cats like to play with me. People use me to knit and crochet. What am I? Draw a picture of me. (*yarn*)

15. I come in dark colors like blue, brown, and gray. People, especially adults, wear me outdoors. I protect their eyes from the sunlight. What am I? Draw a picture of me. (*sunglasses*)

Complete the Sentence

1. At our last club meeting, we discussed [Hmmm].

2. I used the vacuum cleaner to get rid of the [Hmmm].

3. The man sat down on a [Hmmm].

4. She looked up the definition of the word in her [Hmmm].

5. The boys set the table with cups, silverware, and [Hmmm].

6. After a month at sea, the sailors were eager to reach [Hmmm].

7. When the clock struck two, the kids knew it was time to [Hmmm].

8. If you don't do what your teacher tells you to do, you will [Hmmm].

9. The ice made the sidewalk slippery, so the little boy [Hmmm].

10. As the doorbell continued to chime, Shelly hurried to [Hmmm].

11. Kara got her parents' permission to go to the [Hmmm].

12. Beth wanted to write a scary story, so she wrote about [Hmmm].

13. It was raining so hard that the girl wished she had her [Hmmm].

14. My mom stores food in a [Hmmm].

15. Phillip won the race by finishing in less than three [Hmmm].

16. One of the firefighters pointed his hose at the burning [Hmmm].

17. If I had a test coming up this Friday, I would [Hmmm].

18. Douglas brought his favorite snack to share with his class on his [Hmmm].

19. His classmates really enjoyed eating the [Hmmm].

20. When was the last time you took the dog [Hmmm]?

21. As the thunder crashed and the lightning flashed, Grace decided she'd better [Hmmm].

22. Andy invited Joe, Marcy, and Sam to his [Hmmm].

23. I've decided to buy a new [Hmmm].

24. Thank you, Mrs. Andrews, for your help with [Hmmm].

25. The friendly waitress promptly brought us our [Hmmm].

26. Next Friday, May 14, we plan to attend the [Hmmm].

27. As I was leaving for school this morning, I noticed [Hmmm].

28. Jay Martin would like your advice on [Hmmm].

29. Attendance at the carnival was low due to the [Hmmm].

30. The day was damp, gray, and [Hmmm].

Finish the Story

1. Matt and Deb were riding their bikes when suddenly a huge dog came running after them growling and barking loudly. And then . . .

2. Nick and his best friend were walking along the beach collecting seashells when they spotted an old wooden chest that looked as if it had just washed up on the shore. And then . . .

3. E.J. moved closer to the edge of the pond and parted the cattails, looking for the frog. Suddenly, he felt himself begin to slip. And then . . .

4. Trina was walking along the street jingling three quarters in her hand. She had just enough to buy a king-sized candy bar at Herb's Corner Store. A crack in the sidewalk caused her to trip, and one of the quarters fell down a drain grating. And then . . .

5. The children were frightened now that they had lost the paddles. They felt helpless as the stream carried them along. They rounded a bend and smashed into a huge log. And then . . .

6. Jessica gathered up the things she needed to make her dad's surprise birthday cake and took everything up to the cashier. The cashier rang up the purchases and said, "$6.15, please." Jessica looked at the money in her hand with dismay. "I don't have enough," she said. And then . . .

7. Cheryl tried to peer through the pouring rain. It was falling so fast she could barely see four feet ahead of her. Thunder crashed, and the ground she was standing on shook. Lightning flashed all around her. Where was that cabin? If only she could get to it! And then . . .

8. Jeff jumped over the hole and raced toward the chain link fence. He quickly climbed up it and paused at the top just long enough to look back over his shoulder to see if they were still following him. They were; in fact, they were getting closer! And then . . .

9. Feeling desperate, David searched the faces in the crowded amusement park. He ran to the tilt-a-whirl; surely she'd be there! But Rosa was not there. Indeed, it seemed as if his little sister had vanished from the face of the Earth. What would he tell his parents? And then . . .

10. Dawn was almost in tears. How could she get the twins to behave for the next two hours until their parents came home to rescue her? The boys had already eaten worms, run around the outside of the house naked, and called 911. Now they were hiding from her. Suddenly, she heard a loud crash in the garage. And then . . .

Nonsense Sentences

1. Kyle tripped on the stairs and fell up.
2. The volcano spewed smoke, beds, and ashes.
3. Katelyn picked trees to make a bouquet for her grandmother.
4. Their canoe ran into a fly and sank.
5. The fish pulled hard on the clothesline.
6. Jackie retrieved her e-mail with her sewing machine.
7. The man went into the restaurant and ordered jewelry.
8. The family watched football on their stove.
9. I put the cookies into the freezer to bake.
10. Jasmine wanted to play in the snow, so she put on her ballet slippers.
11. The baby drank its milk from a sink.
12. Sara set her new houseplant inside the microwave oven.
13. The boy jumped into the watering can to cool off.
14. The robbers broke into the store to steal dust.
15. The girl used a rake to water her garden.
16. Andrew took the snow shovel and began to mow the lawn.
17. In order to water his lawn, the man turned on his microwave.
18. Brianna used the remote control to change the color of her living room.
19. Sam built a greenhouse so he could raise dolphins.
20. Todd bought a snowblower at the grocery store.
21. Morgan went to computer class to eat.
22. The snowmobile buzzed through the center of the library.
23. Kevin bought his horse at the mall.
24. Since it was July, snow was falling almost every day in New York.
25. Terri made a long distance phone call on her radio.
26. Randy's history report was due the next Sunday.
27. The current prices can only be guaranteed until yesterday.
28. Whenever you want something refreshing to drink, reach for fertilizer.
29. Ben and I will try to meet you at the bottom of the ocean.
30. Tammy used a hammer to mend the tear in her dress.

Which Word Doesn't Belong?

The word that doesn't belong is italicized for each group.

Groups of Four

1. dog, cat, *snake*, mouse
2. leg, arm, eye, *shoe*
3. pool, *prairie*, ocean, pond
4. *ketchup*, diapers, bottle, stroller
5. girl, boy, chicken, *rock*
6. car, *boat*, truck, van
7. boots, socks, slippers, *pants*
8. roses, daisies, *corn*, tulips
9. tub, shower, sink, *bedroom*
10. *sidewalk*, sandbox, swingset, seesaw
11. *curtains*, door, window, roof
12. police officer, *actor*, lifeguard, firefighter
13. teeth, tongue, *lips*, gums
14. turtle, snake, lizard, *rabbit*
15. Saturn, *sun*, Mars, Earth

Groups of Five

1. spring, autumn, summer, *Wednesday*, winter
2. hail, sleet, snow, *drought*, rain
3. *sailor*, boat, ship, raft, canoe
4. ball, *bullet*, bike, slide, swing
5. blue, orange, *three*, yellow, green
6. *shorts*, bat, base, mitt, ball
7. mozzarella, pepperoni, sauce, *frosting*, sausage
8. cherry, apple, *cucumber*, grape, orange
9. skyscrapers, *sheep*, traffic, streets, people
10. *dandelion*, pine, maple, oak, elm
11. desks, books, teachers, homework, *candy*
12. Christmas, Easter, *vacation*, Thanksgiving, Fourth of July
13. hat, boots, coat, scarf, *swimsuit*
14. heart, lungs, *feet*, kidneys, brain
15. microwave, stove, *refrigerator*, toaster, oven

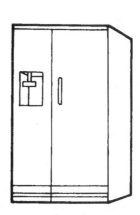

Listen, Then Do

One Step

1. Open the classroom door.
2. Walk up to the board.
3. Take out your pencil.
4. Close the classroom door.
5. Scratch the top of your head.
6. Pull on your left earlobe.
7. Cover your eyes with your hands.
8. Cross your ankles.
9. Fold your arms across your chest.
10. Clap your hands twice.

Two Step

1. Stand up and sit back down.
2. Fold your arms on your desktop and put your head down.
3. Go to the board and write your name.
4. Walk around the room once and then sit in my chair.
5. Stand up and say your name.
6. Flap your arms and make chicken noises.
7. Stand up and lift your right leg as high as you can.
8. Stand up and march in place.
9. Skip to the board and do jumping jacks.
10. Go to a window and march in place.

Three Step

1. Get a book, put it on your head, and walk around the room once.
2. Stand up, close your eyes, and take three steps forward.
3. Stand up, go to the back of the room, and bark like a dog.
4. Jump up and down twice, completely turn around once, and sit back down.
5. Stand up, stamp your feet, and sit on the floor.
6. Walk backwards to my desk, tap my desk four times, and return to your seat.
7. March to the door, say the Pledge, and cross your arms.
8. Stand up, reach both arms over your head, then touch the floor twice.
9. Recite the alphabet, then go to the board, and write your initials.
10. Knock on your desktop three times, then get up and walk around the room twice.

Differentiating Between Fact & Opinion

Prior to doing the famous people, newspaper, or magazine article sections, make sure students can differentiate between fact and opinion. Begin by telling them this story and asking them at the end, sentence by sentence, if each statement is a fact or opinion.

> Wendy looked out the window and said, "It's snowing." (F) Katie rushed over to the window and said, "That's terrific!" (O) "No it's not," said Ken. (O) "I hate snow." (F) Mrs. Carter told them to take their seats. (F) Then she said, "They're forecasting six inches by tomorrow morning." (This one's both: it's a fact that that's the forecast, but the actual amount of snow accumulation is the educated opinion of the weather forecaster.)

Through guided discussion, help students "discover" how certain parts of the story were facts and others were opinions. As a class, brainstorm a list of "signal" words that indicate that something is an opinion. Be sure the following words are included in your signal word list: believes, thinks, best, worst, should, ought.

Next, write the following on the board or overhead:

> **Fact**—something that can be proven true; an actual event or date; well-documented statistics (numbers/percentages)
>
> **Opinion**—what someone thinks/believes; a personal judgment (best, worst, great, terrible)

Leaving the above definitions visible, have the students number a blank sheet of paper from 1 to 10, and then read the following statements aloud to the children. Ask them to write **F** for fact or **O** for opinion after each statement:

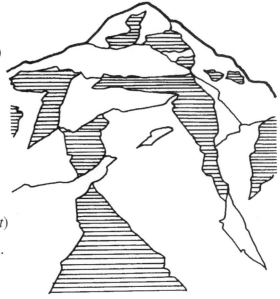

1. The Civil War lasted four years. (*Fact*)

2. Our mayor should be removed from office. (*Opinion*)

3. We usually go to school on Friday. (*Fact*)

4. The United States ought to keep military forces all over the world. (*Opinion*)

5. A short haircut is easier to take care of than a long one. (*Opinion*)

6. Her baby was born on May 1 at 9:20 A.M. (*Fact*)

7. Mt. Everest is the tallest mountain in the world. (*Fact*)

8. YMCA stands for Young Men's Christian Association. (*Fact*)

9. My baby is the most beautiful baby in the world. (*Opinion*)

10. Bach was the best composer who ever lived. (*Opinion*)

Differentiating Between Fact & Opinion *(cont.)*

On another day, with just the definition of **FACT** visible, have the students number a blank sheet of paper from 1 to 10, and then read the following statements aloud. Ask them to write **F** for fact or **O** for opinion after each statement.

1. Michaelangelo painted the ceiling of the Sistine Chapel. *(Fact)*
2. America declared its independence from Britain on July 4, 1776. *(Fact)*
3. Football is the most enjoyable sport to watch. *(Opinion)*
4. You can vote when you turn 18. *(Fact)*
5. It's more important to be good in writing than to excel in sports. *(Opinion)*
6. It's better to live in Dallas than Galveston. *(Opinion)*
7. The President lives in Washington, D.C. *(Fact)*
8. People will never live on Mars. *(Opinion)*
9. Baseball legend Babe Ruth hit 714 home runs during his career. *(Fact)*
10. The Statue of Liberty, which was a gift from France, was finished in 1886. *(Fact)*

On another day, with just the definition of **OPINION** visible, have the students number a blank sheet of paper from 1 to 10, and then read the following statements aloud. Ask them to write **F** for fact or **O** for opinion after each statement.

1. In the United States, women usually live longer than men. *(Fact)*
2. The vehicles Ford makes are better than the ones Dodge makes. *(Opinion)*
3. The state of Florida is larger than Rhode Island. *(Fact)*
4. Americans do not currently recycle enough of their solid waste. *(Opinion)*
5. Former President Theodore Roosevelt had six children. *(Fact)*
6. Abraham Lincoln had a stepmother. *(Fact)*
7. You'll be disappointed if you miss out on seeing the Northern Lights. *(Opinion)*
8. In 1970 the American population was 203,235,298. *(Fact)*
9. Myrtle Beach is not as nice as Virginia Beach. *(Opinion)*
10. The city of Los Angeles lies on the San Andreas fault. *(Fact)*

On another day, without either definition visible, have the students number a blank sheet of paper from 1 to 10, and then read the following statements aloud. Ask them to write **F** for fact or **O** for opinion after each statement.

1. The fashions of the 1990s looked ridiculous. *(Opinion)*
2. The Panama Canal opened on August 15, 1914. *(Fact)*
3. Robin Williams is a hilarious comedian. *(Opinion)*
4. Everyone likes New York state. *(Opinion)*
5. The "Unsinkable" Titanic sunk on her maiden voyage, taking more than 1,500 people with her. *(Fact)*
6. Beatrix Potter's *Peter Rabbit* stories are among the best children's literature ever written. *(Opinion)*
7. Mount Saint Helens erupted in May 1980, destroying everything within a 17-mile radius. *(Fact)*
8. The capital of Pennsylvania is Harrisburg. *(Fact)*
9. It won't rain next Friday. *(Opinion)*
10. The Japanese bombed Pearl Harbor on December 7, 1941. *(Fact)*

Key Words that Signal Important Information

Prior to doing the famous people, newspaper, or magazine article sections, discuss key words with the class and make a bulletin board that should remain up throughout the time you work on listening skills. On the bulletin board, display these key words that signal important information:

- all "-est" words: best, least, fewest, smallest, tallest; most, worst
- an example of
- as a result
- at first
- at last
- because
- caused by
- causing
- characteristics
- chief factors
- compared with
- the definition of
- different kinds of
- dilemma
- the effects
- finally
- for example
- for instance
- in conclusion
- in contrast to
- key reasons

- main causes
- major
- most important
- next
- notice that
- on the other hand
- related to
- remember that
- resulting in
- significant
- some of the reasons
- take note of
- then
- therefore

You may want to include these ideas on the bulletin board, too:

- Write down things that surprise you.
- Write down any "lists" (causes, reasons, steps, achievements).
- Remember that authors often begin and end their writing with their most important ideas—be listening for them!

Folktales
Outline Student Guide

What's Important about a Folktale?

1. Who are the main characters? _____

   _____

   _____

2. Where did it happen? _____

   _____

3. When did it happen? _____

   _____

4. What happened first? _____

   _____

   _____

5. What happened second? _____

   _____

   _____

6. What happened third? _____

   _____

   _____

7. What happened last? _____

   _____

   _____

8. What was the end result? _____

   _____

   _____

9. What did the main character learn as a result? (moral) _____

   _____

   _____

Folktales *(cont.)*
Graphic Organizer

Title		
When?	Characters	
Where?		
Beginning	Middle	End

Moral

Folktales (cont.)

Passage #1

Model the use of the outline on page 18 with this passage.

Here are some words you will need to know as you listen to this folktale:

obstinate: stubborn   **exasperated:** frustrated

The Obstinate Donkey

There once lived a stubborn donkey who never would do as he was told and took great pleasure in being disobedient. When the old widow who owned him wanted him to go to the right, the donkey always pulled to the left. Then when the old widow wanted him to go to the left, he would deliberately pull to the right. Whenever she wanted him to come out of the barn, he refused to leave his stall. When she tried to lead him into the barn to protect him from a coming storm, he refused to enter. In fact, he always tried to do the exact opposite of whatever the old widow said. One day the exasperated old widow thought, "I am getting too old to struggle with this obstinate donkey every single day. I will drive him to market and sell him."

It happened that the way to the village market required the old widow to drive the donkey along a dangerous twisting path that went far up a high mountainside. The donkey knew nothing of her plans to sell him, but when they were very far up, he suddenly decided that he did not want to stay on the path. He turned and ran as fast as he could towards the edge, which was actually a steep cliff. Just as the donkey was just about to pitch head-first over the edge of the cliff, the old widow grabbed him by the tail.

"Come back here, you foolish animal," she cried, tugging on his tail as she gradually backed away up the slope towards the path. "You must come this way, or you'll fall to your death."

"No! No! This way, this way," the donkey stubbornly replied, pulling away from the old widow. "I don't want to go that way."

The donkey pulled with every bit of his might—so hard in fact, that the old widow was forced to let go. The old widow fell down on the grass, and the donkey plunged over the edge of the cliff, braying triumphantly.

Folktales *(cont.)*

Passage #1 Questions

1. Which of the following statements represents the lesson taught in this folktale? Place a checkmark next to one and use it in your answer.

   ❏ If you act foolishly, you may die.

   ❏ It is not wise to be stubborn without a good reason.

   Explain how the story teaches this lesson. Use two details from the folktale to support your answer. (*6 points*)

   _____

   _____

   _____

   _____

   _____

   _____

2. Why did the old widow want to sell her donkey? (*2 points*)

   _____

   _____

   _____

   _____

3. Was either the donkey or the old widow better off by the end of the story than when it started? Explain. (*5 points*)

   _____

   _____

   _____

   _____

4. Give an example of how this folktale could apply to your life. (*2 points*)

   _____

   _____

   _____

   _____

Folktales *(cont.)*

Passage #2

Use the outline on page 18 with this passage.

Here is a word you will need to know as you listen to this folktale:

trio: group of three

The Farmer, His Son, and Their Horse

One day a farmer and his son were walking along a road, leading their horse on a rope. They planned to take him to a neighboring town to sell him. They had not gone very far when they met a group of girls coming from the town, laughing and talking as they walked.

"Just look at that," one of the girls pointed at the trio. "Have you ever seen such foolish people, trudging along the hard road on foot when they could be riding on the back of a horse!"

The father heard what she said, and he whispered to his son to get up on the horse's back. Then they continued on their way, with the boy riding and the father walking along beside him.

Soon they passed a group of old men sitting near the side of the road talking seriously together.

"There's an example right there in front of us!" cried one as the farmer and his son passed by. "The young have no respect for their elders these days. Why, in my youth, you would never see a lazy boy riding a horse while his father walked. Get down from there boy, and let your father rest his legs."

The father heard what he said, and he quietly told his son to get off the horse's back. He mounted the horse himself. Then they continued on their way, this time with the father riding and the boy walking along beside him.

They had only gone a little farther when they encountered a group of women who began whispering, "Have you ever seen such a thing? Just look at that horrible father making his poor little boy trudge along the road while he rides on the horse's back! Why, it's a disgrace!"

The father overheard their whispers and immediately got down off the horse's back.

Then he searched along the roadside until he found a stout pole. Next, he tied the horse's front legs together and back legs together. Finally he tied the horse upside down to the pole. Then the father took one end of the pole and the son took the other, and they went on their way. Shortly thereafter they entered the marketplace, but no one wanted to buy their horse. After all, who would want to purchase a horse that had to be carried to market?

Folktales (cont.)

Passage #2 Questions

1. Which of the following statements represents the lesson taught in this folktale? Place a checkmark next to one and use it in your answer.

   ❏ You should try to make a good impression on other people.

   ❏ Don't let others tell you what to do; think for yourself.

   Explain how the story teaches this lesson. Use two details from the folktale to support your answer. (*6 points*)

   _____

   _____

   _____

   _____

   _____

   _____

2. How does the farmer demonstrate that he cares about making a good impression on other people? (*3 points*)

   _____

   _____

   _____

   _____

3. Why didn't anyone want to buy the horse when they finally reached the market? (*3 points*)

   _____

   _____

   _____

   _____

4. What did you learn about making decisions from this story? (*3 points*)

   _____

   _____

   _____

   _____

Folktales *(cont.)*

Passage #3

Model the use of the folktale graphic organizer on page 19 with this passage.

> Here is a word you will need to know as you listen to this folktale:
>
> **prosper:** do well

The Bundle Of Sticks

There once lived a merchant who was the proud father of three fine sons. However, the sons never stopped quarrelling with one another. The father often told them how much easier life would be if they would work together, but they paid absolutely no attention to his advice.

Finally their constant fighting became more than the merchant could bear, so he devised a plan to show them that they needed to stick together. He called all his sons together and said, "My sons, the time is coming when I will no longer be with you. You will have to run the family business together and must learn to rely on each other. Yet the way the three of you fight, I cannot imagine your working together productively. So do this for me: gather together a bundle of sticks, tie it with string, and bring it here."

When the sons returned with the bundle of sticks, the father said, "Take the bundle just as it is and break it in two. Whichever one of you can do that will inherit everything I own."

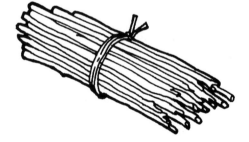

The eldest son tried first. He put his knee on the bundle and pressed and pulled with all his strength, but he could not bend the wood. Then the middle son and finally the youngest son tried, yet each failed. None of them could break the bundle.

"Father, you have given us an impossible task!" they cried. The merchant nodded, then reached for the bundle, undid the string, and removed three sticks, handing one to each son.

"Now try," he said. All three sons easily snapped their sticks across their knees.

Then the merchant asked, "Now do you understand what I mean? When you work together, you will be strong, and your business will prosper. But if you argue and go your separate ways, your enemies may ruin you."

Folktales (cont.)

Passage #3 Questions

1. Which of the following statements represents the lesson taught in this folktale? Place a checkmark next to one and use it in your answer.

   ❏ You shouldn't fight with your brothers (and/or sisters).

   ❏ When we stick together, we are much stronger than we are alone.

   Explain how the story teaches this lesson. Use two details from the folktale to support your answer. (*6 points*)

   _____

   _____

   _____

   _____

   _____

   _____

2. Why do you think the sons argued so much? (*4 points*)

   _____

   _____

   _____

   _____

3. Why was the father so worried about his sons and his business? (*2 points*)

   _____

   _____

   _____

   _____

4. Give an example of how this folktale could apply to your life. (*3 points*)

   _____

   _____

   _____

   _____

Folktales *(cont.)*

Passage #4

Use the folktale graphic organizer on page 19 with this passage.

> Here is a word you will need to know as you listen to this folktale:
>
> **solemnly:** seriously

The Lion and the Wild Boar

One hot day, a thirsty lion and a wild boar came to drink at a pool. Both animals wanted to drink first.

"I got here first. Wait your turn," said the wild boar, standing across the lion's path.

"I am the king of all the beasts," roared the lion. "It is you who should wait your turn. I certainly shouldn't have to wait until you have muddied the water with your hooves."

This angered the wild boar, and he attacked the lion, jabbing at him with his sharp, pointed tusks. The lion lunged at the wild boar's throat, dug in with his teeth, and refused to let go. The brutal sun beat down on the thirsty pair until they could bear no more. They both backed away from each other, panting with exhaustion, one to each side of the pool. As he rested, the lion happened to look up at a nearby rock ledge. There, watching and waiting, sat a crowd of large vultures.

"Look there," he said solemnly to the wild boar. "Those buzzards will eat whichever one of us loses this battle. It matters not to them whether it is me or you. Whoever loses this fight will be finished off in no time."

The wild boar looked up at the birds. Then the lion and the wild boar looked at one another.

"Let's stop fighting," they both said at the same time.

The lion added, "Anything is better than being a vulture's next meal."

The wild boar nodded, saying, "Besides, there is plenty of water here for both of us."

Folktales (cont.)

Passage #4 Questions

1. Which of the following statements represents the lesson taught in this folktale? Place a checkmark next to one and use it in your answer.

   ❑ Enemies will unite against a common enemy.

   ❑ Set aside your differences.

   Explain how the story teaches this lesson. Use two details from the folktale to support your answer. (*6 points*)

   _____

   _____

   _____

   _____

   _____

2. In the beginning, why did the lion insist on drinking first? (*2 points*)

   _____

   _____

   _____

3. How does seeing the vultures change the lion's attitude toward the wild boar? (*4 points*)

   _____

   _____

   _____

4. Who is disappointed by the ending of this story? (*3 points*)

   _____

   _____

   _____

   _____

Folktales *(cont.)*

Passage #5

Do not use student guide pages with this passage.

Here is a word you will need to know as you listen to this folktale:

scrumptious: delicious

The Bees and the Beetle

Once some bees built a large, fine honeycomb filled with incredibly sweet, delicious honey in a hollow tree trunk. You may recall that, in addition to the queen, two different types of bees live in a hive: the worker bees, who spend their lives gathering pollen and making honey, and the drones, who lazily lie around the hive day and night doing absolutely nothing. The drones can't even be bothered with feeding themselves; instead they wait until the workers feed them honey and bee bread.

It happened that the drones began boasting that they had made the finest honeycomb and most scrumptious honey ever seen or tasted in the forest. Their bragging greatly angered the worker bees, so they called in a wise old beetle to decide which bees had built the beautiful honeycomb and made the luscious honey.

"I cannot say for certain which of you built the honeycomb," said the beetle thoughtfully, "for you all look so much alike. However, I have an idea. Why don't you each move to a new location, develop a new hive and build up a new honeycomb. Once the honeycombs are complete, I will inspect them. From the shape of the cells and the taste of the honey I will easily determine who built the fine honeycomb in this hollow tree."

"That's not fair," protested the drone bees. "We don't want to have to build another honeycomb. We are talking about the honeycomb in this hollow tree, not some new honeycomb."

"We'll get started immediately," said the worker bees. "We can probably have it done within twelve days."

The beetle turned to the worker bees and said, "That won't be necessary. Now I know who can make honeycombs and who cannot. Since you are the ones willing and eager to demonstrate your skills, I have no doubt that the fine honeycomb and superb honey in the hollow tree were created by you, the worker bees."

Folktales *(cont.)*

Passage #5 Questions

1. Which of the following statements represents the lesson taught in this folktale? Place a checkmark next to one and use it in your answer.

❑ Your actions are more important than your words.

❑ You shouldn't say you can do something you cannot really do.

Explain how the story teaches this lesson. Use two details from the folktale to support your answer. (*6 points*)

_____

_____

_____

_____

_____

_____

2. Why were the worker bees so angry about the drone bees' bragging? (*3 points*)

_____

_____

_____

3. How did the beetle know for certain which type of bees made the honeycomb and honey? (*4 points*)

_____

_____

_____

4. Give an example of how this folktale could apply to your life. (*2 points*)

_____

_____

_____

_____

Folktales *(cont.)*

Passage #6

Do not use student guide pages with this passage.

Here are some words you will need to know as you listen to this folktale:

conceited: stuck-up, vain   **portion:** part

The Horse and the Overloaded Donkey

There once was a man who owned both a donkey and a horse. The donkey was small, plain, and gray. The horse, a conceited thoroughbred with a sleek, glossy white coat and shining black mane, thought himself much better than the donkey.

When the man went to market to sell his grain, he took both these beasts with him. Onto the tiny donkey's back he loaded all sorts of bags and packages, including the grain he planned to sell, the food they would need on the journey, and gifts for his relatives in town. At last every one of the donkey's saddle bags bulged. The horse's job was only to carry his master. They started out on their way to town, which was about three days' journey away.

Two days later, the donkey struggled up a small rise, straining under the incredibly heavy load while the horse pranced along energetically beside him. The donkey did not feel very well. In fact, he was weakening by the minute and knew he wouldn't make it much farther.

"Please help me, horse," he said. "I don't want you to carry the whole load, but if you would just take a small portion, I know I would manage much better. As it is, I think this burden will be the death of me."

The proud horse refused. "You do your job, and I'll do mine," he said. "Don't bother me with your troubles."

The donkey made no reply and continued on in silence. The sun beat down, and soon his breathing became ragged. Just a short time later, the load overwhelmed him. His legs gave way, and he collapsed in exhaustion in the middle of the road. Although he struggled to stand up, it was obviously impossible. The alarmed owner quickly jumped off the horse's back.

"I can't leave you here," he thought aloud, "and I'll almost certainly miss out on many customers if I wait for you to regain your strength." He looked at the horse. "You're strong enough for two. You'll carry the load for the rest of the way."

To the horse's horror the man removed the heavy bundles from the little donkey and heaved them onto its back. Then he lifted up the donkey and laid it across the horse's saddle as well.

"I'm sorry I didn't helped you when you asked me to," said the horse to the donkey. "Now I must carry not only your load but you as well!"

The worn-out donkey said nothing as he rested all the way to market.

Folktales (cont.)

Passage #6 Questions

1. Which of the following statements represents the lesson taught in this folktale? Place a checkmark next to one and use it in your answer.

    ❏ When you are exhausted, let others help you out.

    ❏ When you don't do your share of the work, you will suffer for it later on.

    Explain how the story teaches this lesson. Use two details from the folktale to support your answer. (*6 points*)

    _____

    _____

    _____

    _____

    _____

    _____

2. Why does the horse say to the donkey, "Don't bother me with your troubles"? (*3 points*)

    _____

    _____

    _____

    _____

3. How would the story probably have changed if the man had waited for the donkey to regain his strength? (*2 points*)

    _____

    _____

    _____

4. Contrast the horse's feelings before and after the donkey falls. (*4 points*)

    _____

    _____

    _____

    _____

Folktales (cont.)

Passage #7

Do not use student guide pages with this passage.

> Here is a word you will need to know as you listen to this folktale:
>
> **rebellion:** an uprising designed to change an existing condition

The Parts of the Body

Long, long ago the parts of the body did not all work together as they do today. Each one had a will and a voice of its own. Eventually, several parts of the body became annoyed with the stomach and started to grumble against him.

"After all, what does he do all day?" said the hands. "We work hard for our living every single moment of every single day, but he just lazily lies there waiting for us to get him good things to eat."

"He's useless as well as lazy," complained the feet. "Every week we walk miles carrying the burden of his weight about."

"Think about us," said the teeth. "We get all worn down chewing up food—just so that he can feel full and satisfied."

"Well, it's gone on long enough," said the hands.

"I agree," said the feet.

"We do, too," said the teeth.

Those three complained so bitterly to the rest of the body that they eventually convinced the rest of the parts of the body to have nothing more to do with the stomach. The feet refused to go to market to purchase food; the hands refused to carry food to the mouth; the mouth refused to allow any food in; the teeth would not chew it—and so on for each part.

Their rebellion had lasted only three days before they all started feeling extremely tired and weak. The feet could barely drag themselves across the ground; the hands shook so much they could scarcely pick up a thing; the teeth ached and grew loose in the gums.

"Well, friends, maybe now you'll face the truth," said the stomach. "Obviously I cannot do anything without you—but how do you feel without me? The simple fact is that none of us can manage without the others." The other parts of the body recognized the truth of what the stomach said and began feeding him once more. Immediately they all started feeling stronger and better.

Ever since that day, the parts of the body have all worked together very well. Occasionally, though, the stomach growls, just to remind the other parts of the body what will happen if they don't feed him. Or perhaps he wants to let the rest of the body know he has never completely forgotten their quarrel.

Folktales *(cont.)*

Passage #7 Questions

1. Which of the following statements represents the lesson taught in this folktale? Place a checkmark next to one and use it in your answer.

   ❑ When everyone works together as a team, things go much better.

   ❑ You should forgive those who have wronged you.

   Explain how the story teaches this lesson. Use two details from the folktale to support your answer. (*6 points*)

   _____

   _____

   _____

   _____

   _____

   _____

2. Why do the other parts of the body stop feeding the stomach? (*5 points*)

   _____

   _____

   _____

   _____

3. How is the body affected when the parts stop feeding the stomach? (*3 points*)

   _____

   _____

   _____

   _____

4. What does the stomach sometimes do to remind the other parts to feed him? (*1 point*)

   _____

   _____

   _____

   _____

Folktales *(cont.)*

Passage #8

Do not use student guide pages with this passage.

Here is a word you will need to know as you listen to this folktale:

regal: royal

The Frogs Get a Ruler

Long ago the frogs decided to ask Mother Nature for a ruler of their own. Mother Nature was amused. So she threw a log of wood into the pond where they lived, saying, "Here you are. Here is a ruler for you."

Because the log made a mighty splash, the frogs dove under the water in fright, burrowing as deep into the mud as they could. After a little while, one of the braver ones swam cautiously to the surface to get a closer look at the new ruler.

"He looks very quiet," thought the frog. "Perhaps he is asleep."

The log stayed quite still on the smooth pond. Eventually, one by one, more frogs came up to take a look. They swam closer and closer. At last a young and impulsive one leaped right on top of it, quite forgetting that he had ever been afraid. Once that happened, other young frogs started using it as a diving board; old frogs sat sunning themselves on it; mother frogs taught their tadpoles how to jump on its bark.

One day an old frog said: "What a dull ruler this is! What we really wanted was someone to keep us in order and make decisions. This one just lies around and lets us do whatever we please." This made the frogs start thinking and discussing what to do. Although several of the frogs protested, the majority of the frogs decided to visit Mother Nature again to request a new ruler.

"Can't you give us a better ruler?" they asked. "Someone who will be a bit more active than the one you sent before?"

Mother Nature felt annoyed by their request. "Those foolish little creatures," she thought. "I shall give them just what they deserve this time."

So she sent a long-legged heron to the pond.

The long-legged heron had a very regal bearing and stood so still and stately that the frogs were immediately very impressed and crowded around it admiringly. But before the frogs could even begin the welcoming speech they had prepared, the heron stuck his long beak into the water and began to swallow every frog within her reach.

"That's not what we meant at all," the frogs shouted to Mother Nature as they dove once more into the mud to hide.

"I only gave you what you asked for," she said. "Perhaps it will teach you not to complain."

And from that day to this frogs live in terror of herons, for a frog is the heron's favorite food.

Folktales *(cont.)*

Passage #8 Questions

1. Which of the following statements represents the lesson taught in this folktale? Place a checkmark next to one and use it in your answer.

   ❏ Be satisfied with what you have.

   ❏ Don't keep asking for favors.

   Explain how the story teaches this lesson. Use two details from the folktale to support your answer. (*6 points*)

   _____

   _____

   _____

   _____

   _____

2. Why did the frogs ask for a ruler in the first place? (*2 points*)

   _____

   _____

   _____

3. What other animals could Mother Nature have sent to the pond as a ruler to teach the frogs a lesson? (*3 points*)

   _____

   _____

   _____

4. What probably would have happened if the frogs had accepted their first ruler? (*4 points*)

   _____

   _____

   _____

   _____

Folktales *(cont.)*

Passage #9

Do not use student guide pages with this passage.

Here are some words you will need to know as you listen to this folktale:

brooding: thinking negative thoughts   **haughty:** proud, arrogant

---

The Owl and the Tiger Lily

One day long ago when the birds were all together, they found a beautiful, perfect tiger lily growing in a meadow. Every bird wanted the tiger lily for itself, so they decided to give it as a prize to the most beautiful of them all. They called together a rabbit, a woodchuck, and a porcupine and asked them to act as judges and decide which bird deserved the gorgeous flower.

One by one each of the birds of the world strutted and flew before the judges. The judges looked at brightly colored cardinals, blue jays, and canaries; snow-white doves; and gleaming black ravens. They saw falcons, eagles, ducks, pheasants, finches, tiny hummingbirds, and many, many more. The judges found it extremely difficult to choose among so many worthy and beautiful birds.

Then an owl came forward. "Let me save you some trouble," he said in a haughty tone. "Obviously I am the most beautiful bird of all. Give me the tiger lily."

The other birds were deeply offended and replied, "The only thing that is obvious is that you are NOT the most beautiful bird of all. Now the sun is setting. Let's all go home and let the judges think about what they have seen overnight. Then they can decide in the morning who shall have the tiger lily."

That night the owl sat on a tree branch brooding. "If they won't give me the prize, then I shall take it for myself," the owl thought. In the darkest part of the night, he silently flew to the tiger lily and took it home.

The next morning the other birds became very angry when they discovered what had happened.

"We must punish that thieving owl," said the robin.

"I think that, since he stole the tiger lily at night, he should never fly in daylight again," said the finch.

"He shall see by night but not by day," added the raven.

"Since he thinks he is so much better than we are, he must live apart from us," said the sparrow.

"So be it," said the eagle.

And that is how the owl became a solitary bird of the night who hides his face all day and flies about only under the cover of darkness.

Folktales *(cont.)*

Passage #9 Questions

1. Which of the following statements represents the lesson taught in this folktale? Place a checkmark next to one and use it in your answer.

   ❑ When you act selfishly, you will eventually suffer.

   ❑ You shouldn't take what isn't yours.

   Explain how the story teaches this lesson. Use two details from the folktale to support your answer. (*6 points*)

   _____

   _____

   _____

   _____

   _____

   _____

2. What two mistakes did the owl make? (*2 points*)

   _____

   _____

   _____

   _____

3. Name the three punishments the owl received. (*3 points*)

   _____

   _____

   _____

   _____

4. What two lessons do you think people would be trying to teach by telling this story? (*4 points*)

   _____

   _____

   _____

   _____

Folktales *(cont.)*

Passage #10

Do not use student guide pages with this passage.

Here are some words you will need to know as you listen to this folktale:

menacing: threatening   **goner:** doomed

The Travelers and the Bear

Once upon a time two men who were best friends went travelling along the road through the woods together. Suddenly a large, growling brown bear came lumbering out of the forest in front of them and blocked their path. Both men were frightened, for neither of them had a weapon. Immediately the bigger, stronger man raced to the nearest sturdy tree and, without giving his friend a second thought, climbed to the upper branches.

The other man knew that he had no chance of defending himself against the menacing bear alone. He remembered hearing that bears never attack a dead body, so he threw himself on the ground and lay as still as possible, pretending to be dead. He held his breath and hoped that the huge bear could not hear his heartbeat, which suddenly seemed exceedingly loud to him. The bear slowly approached him. It grunted in his ear, sniffed and nuzzled around his nose and mouth, and pawed at his backpack. After several minutes of this investigating, the bear whispered something into the man's ear. Then he lumbered down the path, heading away from the two men.

For many minutes the traveler lying on the ground did not dare to move or even look up. Finally he cautiously raised his head and looked about anxiously. He then scrambled to his feet and called to his friend in the tree, "It's safe to come down now."

Still trembling with fear, the friend slowly lowered himself down to the ground.

"Thank heavens you're all right!" he cried. "I was sure you were a goner!" Then he added, "I noticed that the bear put his mouth very close to your ear. Did he whisper a secret to you?"

"Just some friendly advice," replied the other man. "He told me that I should not choose friends who abandon me at the first sign of danger."

Folktales *(cont.)*
Passage #10 Questions

1. Which of the following statements represents the lesson taught in this folktale? Place a checkmark next to one and use it in your answer.

   ❑ A true friend will not desert you even in the face of danger.

   ❑ When you come across a bear in the woods, play dead.

   Explain how the story teaches this lesson. Use two details from the folktale to support your answer. (*6 points*)

   _____

   _____

   _____

   _____

   _____

2. Why do you think the first man acted the way he did? (*2 points*)

   _____

   _____

   _____

   _____

3. Why did the second man behave the way he did? (*4 points*)

   _____

   _____

   _____

4. If he had been a good friend, how would the first man have acted? (*3 points*)

   _____

   _____

   _____

   _____

Folktales *(cont.)*

Passage #11

Do not use student guide pages with this passage.

Here are some words you will need to know as you listen to this folktale:

gore: stab   **brambles:** thorny bushes

The Panther and the Bull

One day, a very hungry panther sat in some bushes watching a fat bull grazing in a field.

"If only he didn't have those sharp horns," thought the panther. "Then I could easily make a feast of him. As it is, he would gore me and then toss me through the air. I could end up dead."

Then he had a clever idea. Quietly slipping up beside the bull, the panther said in a friendly tone, "Excuse me, Mr. Bull, but I just have to say what a handsome beast you are. I've been admiring you, and I must say that I especially like your big, powerful shoulders and strong legs. I am quite curious, though: why on earth do you tolerate those horns on your head? Carrying them around all the time must give you quite a headache; and if I may be so bold as to say so, they do spoil your otherwise perfect appearance."

"Do you really think so?" asked the astonished bull. "Why, I never thought about it. But now that you mention it, these horns often do get in my way. Just last week I even got all tangled up in some brambles because of them. I was trapped for an hour. And they spoil my appearance? Hmmm."

The panther slunk away and hid behind a nearby tree to see what would happen. The bull waited until the panther disappeared from sight, then began hitting his horns against a rock with all his might. After his right horn splintered, he smashed his left horn. Finally, the bull stood up proudly with his head smooth and bare.

"Now I've got you!" snarled the panther as he leapt from his hiding place. "Thank you for destroying your horns. They were the only things that prevented you from becoming my next meal."

Folktales *(cont.)*

Passage #11 Questions

1. Which of the following statements represents the lesson taught in this folktale? Place a checkmark next to one and use it in your answer.

   ❏ Sometimes others say charming things just to get something from you.

   ❏ You should never trust a wild animal.

   Explain how the story teaches this lesson. Use two details from the folktale to support your answer. (*6 points*)

   _____

   _____

   _____

   _____

   _____

2. What was the panther's purpose for telling the bull about his appearance? (*3 points*)

   _____

   _____

   _____

3. Why did the bull deliberately shatter his horns? (*3 points*)

   _____

   _____

   _____

4. What should the bull have done when the panther left him? (*3 points*)

   _____

   _____

   _____

Folktales (cont.)

Passage #12

Do not use student guide pages with this passage.

> Here are some words you will need to know as you listen to this folktale:
>
> **audible:** able to be heard   **devious:** deceptive, dishonest, untrustworthy

The Sick Lion

One day the lion, king of all the beasts, was extremely ill. He did not come out of his cave, but instead lay groaning and murmuring faint, barely audible roars whenever anyone came near.

The other animals did not know what to do. For as long as they could remember the lion had made all their decisions. They had long since forgotten how to think for themselves. After much discussion, they agreed that they must visit him in his cave, for if they stayed away he would certainly be angry and they would suffer upon his recovering. Besides, in his current condition he obviously couldn't harm them even if he wanted to.

So one at a time, or occasionally in small groups, the animals went to the royal cave. Some took him a gift such as the best bit of meat from a recent catch. Others just went to inquire about his health. Large and small, each animal in the lion's kingdom all made their way to his dwelling. However, the fox stayed away. Eventually the lion noticed that the fox never visited him. So the king sent his servant, a hyena, to inquire why the fox was being so rude.

"Fox," said the hyena, "You have displeased His Majesty the lion. Although he is desperately ill, you have not even put your nose inside his cave to ask how he is feeling. What excuse do you have for your disrespectful behavior?"

The fox replied, "Hyena, I would like to see the king, for I respect his wisdom. Indeed, I once came right to the mouth of the cave bearing my best piece of meat as a get-well present."

"And?" the hyena prompted him.

"Although I was anxious to see the king, when I got there I noticed something that made me too frightened to go in," said the fox.

"And what was that?" asked the hyena.

The fox replied, "I saw many pairs of footprints in the sand from all sorts of animals. But they were all going one way—into the cave. Not a single footprint came out. I did not want to enter a place from which I would never return."

The clever fox had figured out the lion's devious plan. Believing he was sick and harmless, the animals he usually had to chase down for food were all coming right into his cave—and ending up as his next meal.

Folktales *(cont.)*
Passage #12 Questions

1. Which of the following statements represents the lesson taught in this folktale? Place a checkmark next to one and use it in your answer.

    ❏ Try to find out the reason someone is acting a certain way.

    ❏ Just because everyone else is doing something, doesn't make it the wise thing to do.

    Explain how the story teaches this lesson. Use two details from the folktale to support your answer. (*6 points*)

    _____

    _____

    _____

    _____

    _____

    _____

2. How is the fox's response different from what the hyena expected? (*4 points*)

    _____

    _____

    _____

    _____

3. What is the fox really trying to say when he tells the hyena, "I didn't want to enter a place from which I wouldn't return"? (*4 points*)

    _____

    _____

    _____

    _____

4. What did you learn about following the crowd from this story? (*1 point*)

    _____

    _____

    _____

    _____

Folktales (cont.)

Use this scoring in conjunction with the answer key to assess student performance.

Scoring Guide			
Points Possible	**Exemplary Score**	**Average Score**	**Minimum Passing Score**
15	12–15	8–11	7

Answer Key

(**Note:** The numbers in parentheses denote points awarded for each correct response.)

Passage #1

1. The lesson this story teaches is that it is unwise to be stubborn for no good reason. (*2 points*) Just to be disobedient, the donkey refuses to go into the barn and so has to stay out in a bad storm (*2 points*). Later the donkey ends up killing himself because he is stubborn. (*2 points*)

2. The old widow wanted to sell her donkey because it refused to do what she wanted it to do. (*2 points*)

3. Neither one was better off at the end. (*1 point*) The donkey died (*2 points*), and the old widow ended up with no donkey to sell (*2 points*).

4. Allow any reasonable responses. Example: If my teacher told me to study and I didn't study, I would probably fail the test. (*1 point*) I would get a bad grade because I was stubborn. (*1 point*)

Passage #2

1. This folktale teaches that you should not let others tell you what to do; you should think for yourself. (*2 points*) The farmer allows people he meets on the way to market to tell him what to do. (*2 points*) He is so eager to please everyone that he ruins his chances of selling his horse at the market. (*2 points*)

2. The farmer tries to please the girls by having his son ride the horse. (*1 point*) He tries to please the old men by riding the horse himself. (*1 point*) He tries to please everyone by carrying the horse into town. (*1 point*)

3. Everyone thought that there must be something wrong with the horse because the farmer and his son carried it into the marketplace. (*2 points*) People wanted to buy a horse to ride, not to carry. (*1 point*)

4. I learned that you must make your own decisions. (*2 points*) If you let everyone else tell you what to do, you may end up doing something foolish. (*1 point*)

Passage #3

1. This story teaches that when we stick together, we can do much more than we can do alone. (*2 points*) The father teaches the sons this by showing them that it is impossible to break a bunch of sticks that are bound together. (*2 points*) Then he shows them that it's very easy to break the same sticks separately. (*2 points*)

2. They each wanted to do things their own way. (*2 points*) They didn't cooperate with each other. (*1 point*) They probably didn't listen to each other's ideas. (*1 point*)

3. The father was worried because if his sons continue to fight all the time, someone could destroy them (*1 point*) or ruin their business. (*1 point*)

4. Allow reasonable responses. Example: If the teacher gave my group a project to do and all we did was argue, we'd never get the project done. (*2 points*) Then we'd all get a bad grade. (*1 point*)

Passage #4

1. This story teaches that enemies will unite against a common enemy. (*2 points*) The wild boar and the lion become enemies because they both want to be the first to drink at the same pool of water. (*2 points*) They stop fighting because their common enemy, the vultures, are waiting to eat whoever loses the fight. (*2 points*)

2. The lion wanted to drink first because he considers himself the king of the beasts (*1 point*), and he wanted to drink before the wild boar muddied the water. (*1 point*)

3. When the lion sees the vultures watching them, the lion changes his attitude from one of proud anger to humble sharing. (*2 points*) He realizes that he wants to stay alive more than he wants to drink first. (*2 points*)

4. The vultures are disappointed. (*2 points*) They had hoped one of the animals would be killed in the fight so they could eat it. (*1 point*)

Answer Key *(cont.)*

Passage #5

1. The lesson this story taught was that actions are more important than words. (*2 points*) The worker bees could actually show that they could make honey and build a honeycomb. (*2 points*) The drone bees refused to show that they could make honey and build a honeycomb because they could not do it, no matter what they said. (*2 points*)

2. The worker bees were angry about the drone bees' bragging because they had worked hard to make the honeycomb and honey, and they didn't want the drones taking the credit for it. (*2 points*) The drone bees never made honey or honeycomb and even made the worker bees wait on them! (*1 point*)

3. The beetle knew that the worker bees made the honeycomb and honey because they were ready and willing to made new ones. (*2 points*) The drones refused to make new ones because they didn't know how. (*2 points*)

4. Allow any reasonable response. Example: If I told someone that I was a terrific hockey player but then I wouldn't play hockey in front of him, he probably wouldn't believe me. (*1 point*) Because I would not show my playing, he wouldn't think I was telling the truth about being a terrific player. (*1 point*)

Passage #6

1. This story taught that when you don't do your share of the work, you will suffer for it later on. (*2 points*) The horse refuses to help the donkey carry even part of his heavy load. (*2 points*) When the donkey falls, the horse ends up carrying the whole load plus the donkey. (*2 points*)

2. The horse thinks that he is superior to the donkey (*1 point*) and doesn't want to help the donkey at all. (*2 points*)

3. If the man had waited for the donkey to regain his strength, the donkey probably would have had to carry the load all the way to town (*1 point*), and the horse wouldn't have learned his lesson. (*1 point*)

4. Before the donkey falls, the horse couldn't care less about the donkey's suffering. (*2 points*) After the donkey falls, the horse wishes he had helped the donkey because now he is suffering. (*2 points*)

Passage #7

1. This story teaches that when everyone works together as a team, things go much better. (*2 points*) When the parts of the body stop working together and refuse to feed the stomach, they all start to feel weak and unhealthy. (*2 points*) When the parts of the body start working together by feeding the stomach, they all begin feeling stronger and healthier. (*2 points*)

2. They do not realize that the stomach is doing an important job. (*2 points*) They believe that the stomach is just being lazy (*2 points*) and waiting for them to take care of its needs. (*1 point*)

3. The feet can barely walk. (*1 point*) The hands shake. (*1 point*) The teeth ache and get loose. (*1 point*)

4. The stomach makes grumbling noises to remind the other parts to feed him. (*1 point*)

Passage #8

1. The story teaches you to be satisfied with what you have. (*2 points*) The frogs request a ruler but don't like it when the ruler does nothing. (*2 points*) They ask for a another ruler, and this one terrorizes them by eating them. (*2 points*)

2. They wanted someone to tell them what to do (*1 point*) and make decisions for them. (*1 point*)

3. Mother Nature could have sent a snapping turtle (*1 point*), a snake (*1 point*), or bird of prey (*1 point*). (Allow any three reasonable responses.)

4. The frogs would have lived peacefully without fear. (*2 points*) They could have learned to make their own decisions. (*2 points*)

Folktales *(cont.)*

Answer Key *(cont.)*

Passage #9

1. This story teaches that when you act selfishly, you will eventually suffer. (*2 points*) The owl acted selfishly when he took the tiger lily (*2 points*), but then the other animals punished him for doing it. (*2 points*)

2. He assumed he was the most beautiful bird (*1 point*), and he stole the tiger lily. (*1 point*)

3. The owl can only see well at night. (*1 point*) The owl doesn't fly during the day. (*1 point*) The owl must live apart from the other birds. (*1 point*)

4. They would be trying to teach people not to steal (*2 points*) and not to act selfishly. (*2 points*)

Passage #10

1. This folktale teaches that a true friend will not desert you even in the face of danger. (*2 points*) The bear tells this to the man on the ground. (*2 points*) The first man is not a true friend because he only thinks about his own safety and does nothing to help the man on the ground. (*2 points*)

2. He was probably afraid that the bear would kill him. (*1 point*) He thought that he would be safer up a tree than on the ground. (*1 point*)

3. He couldn't fight the bear alone. (*1 point*) He didn't want the bear to eat him. (*1 point*) He pretended to be dead because he had heard that a bear will not eat a dead body. (*2 points*)

4. He would have tried to defend himself and his friend. (*2 points*) Perhaps together they could have driven the bear off. (*1 point*)

Passage #11

1. This story teaches that sometimes others say charming things just to get something from you. (*2 points*) In the conversation between a bull and a panther, the panther tells the bull that he is beautiful except that his horns ruin his appearance. (*2 points*) In truth, the panther just wants the bull to get rid of the horns so he can attack and eat him. (*2 points*)

2. The panther wanted to charm the bull into thinking that he would look better without horns so that the bull would get rid of his horns. (*2 points*) The panther wanted the bull to have no horns because the panther was afraid of being injured by them. (*1 point*)

3. The panther said they ruined his appearance (*1 point*) and the bull believed the panther. (*1 point*) The bull wanted to be better-looking. (*1 point*)

4. The bull should have ignored the panther's comments. (*1 point*) The bull should have realized that he looks the way a bull is supposed to look. (*2 points*)

Passage #12

1. This folktale teaches that just because everyone else is doing something, doesn't make it the right thing to do. (*2 points*) All the other animals are visiting the lion, and the fox is pressured by the hyena to visit, too. (*2 points*) The fox wisely refuses because he realizes that the animals are being eaten by the lion. (*2 points*)

2. The hyena expects the fox to apologize (*1 point*) and go to see the lion immediately (*1 point*). Instead, the fox tells the hyena that he knows that the sick lion is up to something. (*2 points*)

3. The fox really means that he doesn't want to end up as the lion's meal. (*2 points*) He is telling the hyena that he has figured out the lion's evil plan. (*2 points*)

4. I learned that following the crowd can be dangerous. (*1 point*)

Literature Selections
Outline Student Guide

What's Important about Literature?

Title: _____ Author: _____

1. Major characters (concentrate on the most important, up to three):

   _____

   _____

2. Historical time period:_____

   _____

3. Place where it happened:_____

   _____

4. What is the main problem (conflict)? _____

   _____

5. What happened first? _____

   _____

6. What happened second? _____

   _____

7. What happened third? _____

   _____

8. What happened last? _____

   _____

9. What was the end result (problem's resolution)? _____

   _____

10. How did the main character change? What did the main character learn as a result?

   _____

   _____

   _____

Literature Selections *(cont.)*
Graphic Organizer

Title: _____ Author: _____

Setting:
| When: |
| Where: |

Characters: _____

_____

_____

Main Problem:
(Conflict)

Event 1: _____

Event 2: _____

Event 3: _____

Event 4: _____

Event 5: _____

End result:

Effect on
main
character:

Literature Selections (cont.)

The literature selections were made based on a variety of factors—the main ones being that they are quality literature and common enough that they should be readily available to you in your school or public library. Do not show the students any illustrations, including the front cover of the book. You can place the book within a pocket folder when you read it aloud to the students or record the passage on a cassette tape to play for the students.

Note: The following Reading Levels were obtained from *The Elementary School Library Collection*. Since the passages increase in difficulty, read them in the order presented. The level of difficulty was determined by taking into account not only the reading level but also the complexity of the passage and the questions asked about it. Also, the most challenging passages were deliberately placed at the beginning where students will receive instructor modeling and support from the student guide pages.

Literature Passage #1

Model the use of the outline on page 47 for this passage.

Book: *A Wrinkle in Time* by Madeleine L'Engle

Reading Level: 6.5

Show the children a circle drawn on a sheet of paper and a ball and explain to them how one is two-dimensional and the other is three-dimensional. Explain that everything on Earth is either two- or three-dimensional. Ask them whether they themselves are two- or three-dimensional. Then read the passage about the children being transported through the fifth dimension, beginning in chapter 5 with "Well, the fifth dimension's a tesseract . . ." and end by reading the paragraph, "Meg looked around her, realizing that she had been so . . ."

Here are some words you will need to know as you listen to this passage:

tesseract: an imaginary word for wrinkle

corporeal: of the physical body

illuminating: promoting understanding, shedding light onto something

dissolution: disintegrating into many parts

intolerable: not able to be put up with

protoplasm: a substance in the cells of all plants and animals

Literature Passage #2

Use the outline on page 47 for this passage.

Book: *A Gathering of Days: A New England Girl's Journal, 1830-1832* by Joan Blos

Reading Level: 7.0

Read the diary entries beginning with Wednesday, December 1, 1830, and stop after reading the journal entry dated Sunday, December 12, 1830.

Here are some words you will need to know as you listen to this passage:

transpired: happened

foolscap pages: odd-sized paper

scholar: one who studies

disported: entertained

mayhap: perhaps

befallen: happened to

contrived: made an effort

mortification: extreme embarrassment

pantaloons: girls' underwear that reaches to the ankles

indenture: a contract where one person serves another for a period of time (usually years)

Literature Selections *(cont.)*

Literature Passage #3

Model the use of the graphic organizer on page 48 for this passage.

Book: *Dragon's Gate* by Laurence Yep

Reading Level: 6.6

Read chapter 12 in which the Chinese laborers set charges to blow up part of the mountain.

Here are some words you will need to know as you listen to this passage.

T'ang people: Chinese
the Tiger: a mountain
hazing: tormenting
brusquely: bluntly, harshly

westerners: Americans
stifling: suffocating
ventilation: bringing in fresh air
preoccupied: thinking about something else

Literature Passage #4

Use the graphic organizer on page 48 for this passage.

Book: *Holes* by Louis Sachar

Reading Level: 6.0

Read the passage about Stanley and Zero finding the suitcase. Begin in chapter 44 with paragraph "It was so dark . . ." and end in chapter 45 with "Three other counselors . . ."

Here are some words you will need to know as you listen to this passage.

swig: big swallow
spigot: faucet
pronounced: obvious

precarious: dangerous
illuminated: lighted
commotion: upset

Literature Passage #5

Do not use the student guide pages for this passage.

Book: *Bunnicula* by James and Deborah Howe

Reading Level: 5.2

Read about the white tomato. Read from "'You fell asleep?" to the end of chapter 3.

Here are some words you will need to know as you listen to this passage:

proceedings: happenings

reverie: daydreaming

Literature Passage #6

Do not use the student guide pages for this passage.

Book: *The Whipping Boy* by Sid Fleischman

Reading Level: 4.0

Read chapters 2 through 4 in which Jemmy is beaten for Prince Brat's offense and Prince Brat and Jemmy run away and are captured by cutthroats.

Here are some words you will need to know as you listen to this passage:

chamber: bedroom
scragged: hung by the neck
insolent: rude

thrashed: whipped
gallows: a platform used to hang people
cutthroat: criminal

Literature Selections (cont.)

Do not use the student guide pages for this passage.

Book: *Felita* by Nicholasa Mohr

Reading Level: 4.0

Read the passage where Felita and her grandmother discuss how Felita was verbally assaulted, beginning in chapter 3 with the paragraph that begins, "Now, mi Felita. Do you want to hear a story?" and finishing with Felita saying, "I understand, Abuelita." The Spanish pronunciations are: **abuelita** = ab-well-EE-tuh; **Tio** = TEE-oh; and **Jorge** = HOR-hey (Hispanic version of George).

Here are some words you will need to know as you listen to this passage:

tio: uncle

abuelita: grandmother

ignorant: uneducated

ignoramuses: stupid people

Literature Passage #8

Do not use the student guide pages for this passage.

Book: *On My Honor* by Marion Bauer

Reading Level: 5.3

Read the passage about the teenage boy searching the river for Tony, beginning in chapter 6 with, "'Please,' Joel gasped, but then he couldn't say any more . . ." and finishing with the end of chapter 6.

Here are some words you will need to know as you listen to this passage:

stifled: muffled

sandbar: a raised patch of sand in a body of water

sheeting off: flowing from

shear off: remove

reverberated: echoed

Literature Passage #9

Do not use the student guide pages for this passage.

Book: *Julie of the Wolves* by Jean Craighead George

Reading Level: 6.4

Read the passage about Julie leaving her father to live in the village with her Aunt Martha, beginning in Part 2 with the words, "Summers at seal camp were not as beautiful . . ." and finish by reading the paragraph that begins "The next year Julie worked at the hospital. . . ."

Here are some words you will need to know as you listen to this passage:

kayak: one-person boat

pinched: strained

oilskin: a type of waterproof cloth

bladder bag: pouch made from an animal's bladder

derisively: mockingly

trough: the low area between waves

Literature Selections *(cont.)*

Literature Passage #10

Do not use the student guide pages for this passage.

Book: *Sounder* by William Armstrong

Reading Level: 6.9

Read the passage about Sounder being shot by the sheriff, beginning in chapter 2 with the words "'Get up,' said the second man," and finishing with "Maybe his father had said it hurt to bounce. . . ."

Here are some words you will need to know as you listen to this passage:

ashen: pale gray

mongrel: mutt

smokehouse: shed where meat is smoked and stored so it won't spoil

ticking: a strong cotton fabric

lunge: sudden leap forward

Literature Passage #11

Do not use the student guide pages for this passage.

Book: *Roll of Thunder, Hear My Cry* by Mildred Taylor

Reading Level: 7.0

Read the passage in chapter 3 about how the children get splashed by the school bus, beginning with these words: "If we had been faced only with the prospect of the rain soaking through our clothing . . ." and finishing by reading the paragraph "Finally, when the bus was less than fifty feet . . ."

Here are some words you will need to know as you listen to this passage:

prospect: possibility

embittered: resentful

gullies: ditches

inaccessible: unable to be reached

dejected: very unhappy

sodden: soaked

Literature Passage #12

Do not use the student guide pages for this passage.

Book: *Tuck Everlasting* by Natalie Babbit

Reading Level: 6.3

Read in chapter 12 the section where Tuck describes his plight to Winnie, starting with "Here and there the still surface of the water . . ." and finish by reading the paragraph that begins "There was a long, long moment. . . ."

Here are some words you will need to know as you listen to this passage:

stern: rear part of a boat

brambles: bushes with thorns

slops: pig food

pinched: strained

rigid: stiff

anguish: suffering

Literature Selections *(cont.)*

Literature Passage #1 Questions

Based on the passage you just heard, answer these questions about *A Wrinkle In Time* with as much detail as possible.

1. Thoroughly describe Meg's experience of moving through the fifth dimension. (*8 points*)

_____

_____

_____

_____

_____

_____

2. What does Mrs. Which do that almost kills the children? (*5 points*)

_____

_____

_____

_____

3. Once she has passed through the time travel, who does Meg see on the new planet? (*5 points*)

_____

_____

_____

_____

4. What did Mrs. Whatsit do to keep Meg's mother from worrying about her while she's gone? (*2 points*)

_____

_____

_____

_____

Literature Selections (cont.)

Literature Passage #2 Questions

Based on the passage you just heard, answer these questions about *A Gathering of Days: A New England Girl's Journal, 1830-1832* with as much detail as possible.

1. According to Catherine's journal, what do the children do to entertain themselves after school? (*2 points*)

   _____

   _____

2. How does Catherine's school book get returned to her? Is it the same as when she last saw it? (*4 points*)

   _____

   _____

   _____

3. Describe the message Catherine gets in a secret note. Where does she find it, and who wrote the note? What does it say? (*4 points*)

   _____

   _____

   _____

4. What do Asa and Catherine think is going on based on Catherine's book and Asa's discovery in the woods? (*7 points*)

   _____

   _____

   _____

   _____

5. After Asa shares his discovery, why does Catherine struggle to decide what's the right thing to do? (*3 points*)

   _____

   _____

   _____

Literature Selections (cont.)

Literature Passage #3 Questions

Based on the passage you just heard, answer these questions about *Dragon's Gate* with as much detail as possible.

1. Does Otter understand what's happening when Uncle Foxfire cries, "Fire in the heading?" What does he do? (*4 points*)

   _____

   _____

   _____

2. Explain in detail the task that the workers in the story are doing. How much progress do they make each day? (*6 points*)

   _____

   _____

   _____

   _____

3. Name four of the difficulties and dangers the workers face on the mountain. (*4 points*)

   _____

   _____

   _____

   _____

4. What does Bright Star catch Doggy doing? What does Bright Star make him do? (*2 points*)

   _____

   _____

   _____

5. Is Kilroy satisfied with the amount of progress they made that day with the mountain? How do you know? (*4 points*)

   _____

   _____

   _____

Literature Selections (cont.)

Literature Passage #4 Questions

Based on the passage you just heard, answer these questions about *Holes* with as much detail as possible.

1. Why were Stanley and Zero digging in the dark? What did they hope to find? (*4 points*)

   _____

   _____

   _____

2. What happens when Stanley finds something in the hole? What exactly did he find? (*8 points*)

   _____

   _____

   _____

   _____

3. What clues let you know that all the people are afraid of the lizards? What's probably the reason that they're afraid? (*5 points*)

   _____

   _____

   _____

   _____

4. Who do you think was hoping that Stanley and Zero would find something? Why do you think so? (*3 points*)

   _____

   _____

   _____

   _____

Literature Selections (cont.)
Literature Passage #5 Questions

Based on the passage you just heard, answer these questions about *Bunnicula* with as much detail as possible.

1. What startling discovery does Mr. Monroe make, and what is his wife's explanation for it? (*2 points*)

   _____

   _____

   _____

2. Using clues from the story, describe the characters Chester, Harold, and Bunnicula. (*5 points*)

   _____

   _____

   _____

   _____

3. What does Chester believe happened during the night? Why does he think so? (*7 points*)

   _____

   _____

   _____

   _____

4. Harold is polite while listening to Chester's theory, but what is he actually more interested in? What does he do? (*3 points*)

   _____

   _____

   _____

5. Who do you think Toby and Peter are? How do you know? (*3 points*)

   _____

   _____

   _____

Literature Selections *(cont.)*

Literature Passage #6 Questions

Based on the passage you just heard, answer these questions about *The Whipping Boy* with as much detail as possible.

1. Tell everything that happens when Prince Brat doesn't know his lessons. (*5 points*)

   _____

   _____

   _____

   _____

2. Explain in detail why having a whipping boy is ridiculous. (*3 points*)

   _____

   _____

   _____

3. What does Jemmy think when he finds out that the prince wants to run away? (*4 points*)

   _____

   _____

   _____

4. Where does Jemmy think about running away to? Once there, how does he plan to make money? (*3 points*)

   _____

   _____

   _____

5. Describe how Jemmy and the prince are captured. (*5 points*)

   _____

   _____

   _____

   _____

Literature Selections *(cont.)*

Literature Passage #7 Questions

Based on the passage you just heard, answer these questions about *Felita* with as much detail as possible.

1. What do you think the girls probably said to Felita that made her so upset? (*4 points*)

   _____

   _____

   _____

2. What are the two main points that Abuelita wants Felita to know about all Puerto Ricans? (*3 points*)

   _____

   _____

   _____

3. What does Abuelita tell Felita to do from now on when she meets people who say nasty things to her? (*5 points*)

   _____

   _____

   _____

   _____

4. Abuelita tells Felita, "Even the rich and powerful use the bathroom, just like you and me." What does she really mean? (*5 points*)

   _____

   _____

   _____

   _____

5. Explain the three things about all people that Felita's grandmother thinks are the most important for her to remember. (*3 points*)

   _____

   _____

   _____

Literature Selections *(cont.)*

Literature Passage #8 Questions

Based on the passage you just heard, answer these questions about *On My Honor* with as much detail as possible.

1. When he was leading the teenagers to the river, what made Joel collapse? (*4 points*)

   _____

   _____

   _____

2. What does the teenager say when Joel tells him that he can't quit searching for Tony? (*5 points*)

   _____

   _____

   _____

3. What frightens Joel about going to the police? (*2 points*)

   _____

   _____

   _____

4. Besides the police, who are the other people Joel is afraid to tell? Why? (*4 points*)

   _____

   _____

   _____

   _____

5. Do you think it was strange that the teenagers left it up to Joel to report what had happened to the police? Explain why. (*5 points*)

   _____

   _____

   _____

   _____

Literature Selections *(cont.)*

Literature Passage #9 Questions

Based on the passage you just heard, answer these questions about *Julie of the Wolves* with as much detail as possible.

1. Describe Julie's life with her father during the summer in the seal camp. Was she happy there? (*4 points*)

   _____

   _____

   _____

   _____

2. Explain the circumstances that force Julie and her father to be separated. (*4 points*)

   _____

   _____

   _____

   _____

3. What does Kapugen tell Julie to do in case she is unhappy at Aunt Martha's? (*3 points*)

   _____

   _____

   _____

4. Does Julie try to fit in with the Americanized Eskimos? How? (*5 points*)

   _____

   _____

   _____

5. What happens when Julie compliments Judith's i'noGo tied? (*4 points*)

   _____

   _____

   _____

   _____

Literature Selections *(cont.)*

Literature Passage #10 Questions

Based on the passage you just heard, answer these questions about *Sounder* with as much detail as possible.

1. How is the boy's father arrested? What do they think he did? (*5 points*)

   _____

   _____

   _____

   _____

2. The deputy says to the man, "You gonna wear nothing but stripes pretty soon. Big, wide black and white stripes. Easy to hit with a shotgun." What does the deputy mean? (*4 points*)

   _____

   _____

   _____

3. What happens when Sounder finally realizes that there are strangers in the house? (*4 points*)

   _____

   _____

   _____

4. Why did Sounder chase after the wagon? How did he get loose? (*4 points*)

   _____

   _____

   _____

5. Why is the boy afraid for his father's life? (*3 points*)

   _____

   _____

   _____

   _____

Literature Selections (cont.)

Literature Passage #11 Questions

Based on the passage you just heard, answer these questions about *Roll of Thunder, Hear My Cry* with as much detail as possible.

1. Why do Cassie, her brothers, and their friends walk to school every day, even in the bad weather? (*4 points*)

   _____

   _____

2. What does the Jefferson Davis School bus driver often do to Cassie and the other children who walk with her to school? (*3 points*)

   _____

   _____

3. What really makes Little Man so upset about the fact that each day his clothes get so dirty? (*3 points*)

   _____

   _____

   _____

4. How would Big Ma be likely to react if Little Man told her that black students get the torn, worn-out textbooks that the white students refuse to use? What would she probably say? (*3 points*)

   _____

   _____

   _____

5. Explain in detail what Cassie, Christopher John, Little Man, Stacey, Claude, and T. J. do to avoid the bus as they walk to school on a soggy, rainy morning. What happens to them in the end? (*7 points*)

   _____

   _____

   _____

   _____

Literature Selections *(cont.)*

Literature Passage #12 Questions

Based on the passage you just heard, answer these questions about *Tuck Everlasting* with as much detail as possible.

1. What is so unusual about the Tucks? Be specific. (*2 points*)

   _____

   _____

   _____

2. When he talks to Winnie, does Tuck sound like he enjoys being different? Why? (*5 points*)

   _____

   _____

   _____

3. Does Tuck want the people in Treegap to know about the spring? Why? (*4 points*)

   _____

   _____

   _____

4. Explain how Tuck describes life as being like a wheel. (*5 points*)

   _____

   _____

   _____

   _____

5. What is Winnie thinking and feeling during her talk with Tuck? (*4 points*)

   _____

   _____

   _____

   _____

Literature Selections (cont.)

Use this scoring guide in conjunction with the answer key to assess student performance.

Scoring Guide			
Points Possible	**Exemplary Score**	**Average Score**	**Minimum Passing Score**
20	17–20	14–16	12

Answer Key

(**Note:** The numbers in parentheses denote points awarded for each correct response.)

Passage #1: *A Wrinkle in Time*

1. Meg feels a gust of wind, a big push, and a sharp shattering (1); then there is darkness and silence (1). Her body seems to dissolve (1), and she can't feel Calvin's hand (1). She then feels as if she's being squashed (1); it's also hard to breathe and think (1). Next, she goes back into the darkness and silence (1). Finally, she feels the tingling come back into her fingers as her body comes back to normal (1).

2. She takes them to a two-dimensional planet (1), where they become flat (1). Since the children are three-dimensional (1), they are unable to breathe (1) and their hearts can't beat (1).

3. On the new planet, Meg sees Charles Wallace (1), Calvin (1), Mrs. Who (1), Mrs. Whatsit (1), and an occasional glimmer of Mrs. Which (1).

4. To be sure that Meg's mom wouldn't worry, Mrs. Whatsit created a time wrinkle (1). When the children return from this adventure, they'll arrive five minutes before they ever left (1).

Passage #2: *A Gathering of Days*

1. They go skating on a frozen pond (1); the boys pull the girls around on the ice on pine branches (1).

2. Her missing book reappears on a rock (1) between the schoolhouse and the woods (1). It is obvious that someone took it and deliberately wrote in it (1). The writer asks her to have pity because he is cold (1).

3. Catherine finds a note hidden under a rock in her front yard (1). Though the note isn't signed, she knows it's from Asa (1). He tells her to wait at the rock (1), but he doesn't say which rock or when (1).

4. Someone took the book and wrote for help in it (1). When Asa discovers a man's footprints in the woods (1), he and Catherine believe that the man who wrote in the book is hiding there (1). They think that he's a black man (1) who is either a runaway slave (1), a thief (1), or an escaped convict (1).

5. Catherine doesn't know if she should help the runaway (1)—she's not sure if he is an escaped slave or an escaped convict (1). She would be willing to help an escaped slave, but not a criminal (1).

Passage #3: *Dragon's Gate*

1. No, Otter doesn't understand what's happening (1). He keeps filling his basket (1) until his father rushes to him (1) and hurries him out of the mountain (1).

2. The workers are digging holes in a mountain (1) and filling them with explosives (1), which are then lit (1). This blows away a tiny part of the mountain (1). The rubble is removed, placed in baskets, and carried out of the mountain (1). They progress less than one foot each day (1).

3. The air inside the mountain is hard to breathe (1). It's very cold (1), and the work is tiring (1). Workers have lost body parts due to the explosions (1). The crew members don't get along (1). They make very little progress for all their hard work each day (1). (Any 4 = 4 pts.)

4. Bright Star catches Doggy stealing Otter's glove (1). He makes him return it (1).

5. At first Kilroy seems satisfied with the progress they made that day (1), but then he tells Uncle Foxfire to double charge the holes the next day (1). Kilroy says he doesn't like the orders any better than they do (1), but that they need to catch up to the schedule (1).

Passage #4: *Holes*

1. They were digging in the dark because they did not want to be seen (1). They hoped to find a chest (1) filled with jewels (1) that Kate Barlow (1) buried.

2. He finds a suitcase (1). As he lifts it out of the hole and hands it to Zero (1), a light shines in his eyes (1). The Warden (1), Mr. Pendaski (1), and Mr. Sir (1) are standing there (1). Also, the hole is full of lizards, which are crawling on Zero and Stanley (1).

3. The Warden stops talking and moving when she sees one (1), Zero sits as still as a statue (1), and Stanley tries to stay still (1). Also, one counselor whispers, "Oh my God . . ." when she sees them (1). They're probably afraid that the lizards are poisonous (1).

4. The Warden was hoping that Stanley and Zero would find the treasure chest (1). She doesn't even ask what they've discovered; she seems to already know (1). She thanks the boys for being very helpful (1).

Literature Selections *(cont.)*

Answer Key *(cont.)*

Passage #5: *Bunnicula*

1. Mr. Monroe discovers a white tomato in the refrigerator (1). His wife cuts it open to make sure that it is a tomato, then says it's gone bad (1).

2. Chester is a cat (1) who believes a vampire attacked the tomato (1). Harold is a dog (1) who is telling the story (1), and Bunnicula is a pet rabbit (1).

3. Chester thinks that Bunnicula got out of his cage (1), went into the fridge (1), and sucked the color out of a tomato (1). During the night, Chester saw the light go out in the kitchen (1) and Bunnicula come out shortly after that (1). The next day a tomato is found that is white (1) and has bite marks on it (1).

4. Harold knows that the Monroes are cooking bacon (1), and he is interested in getting some to eat (1). Even though he listens to what Chester thinks, he runs back into the kitchen the minute he hears the sound of bacon crunching (1).

5. Peter and Toby are the Mr. and Mrs. Monroe's sons (1). I know this because Peter calls Mr. Monroe dad (1) and Chester jumps up on Toby's shoulders like he's a family member (1).

Passage #6: *The Whipping Boy*

1. When Prince Brat doesn't know his lessons, his tutor gets very upset and yells at him (1). Then the tutor says he must be punished (1). The prince suggests 10 hard whacks (1), but instead of taking the punishment himself, a whipping boy named Jemmy receives the blows (1). Then the prince complains because the boy takes the beating without crying or making any noise (1).

2. It is ridiculous because the prince can do anything he wants and Jemmy will always be the one punished for it (1). Since he doesn't care if Jemmy is beaten, the prince has no motivation to improve his behavior (1). So, his behavior just gets worse (1).

3. He can't understand why the prince would want to leave his privileged life (1) with guaranteed food and shelter. Jemmy often thought about running away, but he had a good reason (1) because he was tired of being whipped for Prince Brat's misbehavior (1). He is amazed by the prince's excuse of being bored (1).

4. He thinks about running away to live in the sewers (1). His father taught him how to move around through them, so he thought no one would find him there (1). He planned to catch rats to sell to the people who hold rat fights (1).

5. Jemmy had gotten down from the horse at the prince's command, but instead of leading the horse, he began tiptoeing away (1). Just then the prince started shouting (1). One criminal grabbed the prince on the horse (1) and another surprised Jemmy by grabbing his arm (1). The two boys didn't see the men approach because of the dense fog (1).

Passage #7: *Felita*

1. They probably made fun of Felita's appearance (1) and her family (1). They probably said that Felita and her family weren't as good as them (1) and tried to make her feel bad about being Puerto Rican (1).

2. Abuelita wants Felita to know that Puerto Ricans are a mixture of all the races in the world (1). She tells Felita that Puerto Ricans are American citizens (1) and therefore have every right to be in America (1).

3. She tells Felita to tell the people that all Puerto Ricans are American citizens (1) and are a part of all races (1). She says Felita should tell people that she has an advantage because she knows two languages (1). When people gang up on Felita, Abuelita wants her to walk away (1) rather than try to retaliate (1).

4. Abuelita means that all people are essentially the same no matter what they look like (*2 points*). All people have the same feelings and needs (1), no matter how different they seem. Even if a person is rich or powerful, he is still just a human being (1) who eats, sleeps, and goes to the bathroom (1).

5. Felita's grandmother wants Felita to remember that everyone has the same emotions and needs (1). Everyone can feel sorrow or be hurt by others (1), and no one is better because of their skin or hair (1).

Passage #8: *On My Honor*

1. Joel collapsed as soon as he saw the river (1) and smelled the water (1). He remembered how the river had almost drowned him (1), and he was horrified because Tony was lost somewhere in that river (1).

2. The teenager tells Joel that Tony has drowned (1). He explains that it takes just five minutes to drown (1), and it has been much longer than that since Tony disappeared (1). The teen also points out that the current of the river is so swift that the body probably won't be found for a week or more (1). He tells Joel he's sorry and says they need to tell the police (1).

3. Joel is afraid the police will ask why he and Tony were swimming in the river (1). Joel also thinks that the police will blame him for losing his friend (1).

4. Joel doesn't want to tell his father (1) because he had promised him that he and Tony would only go to the state park (1). He doesn't want to think about the look on Tony's mother's face when she finds out (1). Joel is also terrified that Tony's father will beat him with a belt (1) when he finds out what happened.

5. Yes, it was strange (1). A drowning is an emergency (1), and Joel is just a kid (1). Also, he has a bicycle and is miles from a phone (1). The teens, being in a car, could have gotten help faster (1) **OR** No, it wasn't strange (1). Joel promised he would report it (1), and they had no reason not to believe him (1). Also, the girl was afraid of getting in trouble at her job (1). She had called in sick to work so she could spend the day with her boyfriend (1).

Literature Selections (cont.)

Answer Key (cont.)

Passage #9: *Julie of the Wolves*

1. Julie is very happy with her father in the seal camp (1). Whenever her father was gone, she played with other children on the beach, dug for clams, and ate prickly sea urchins (any 2 = 2 pts.). In the summer, many Eskimos came who spoke English. They called her Julie instead of her Eskimo name (1).

2. Julie's Aunt Martha comes and tells her father that Julie must go to school (1). There is a law that says Julie must attend because she is 9 years old. (1). In addition, her father is being called into service because of a war (1) and cannot leave Julie alone, so he agrees to let her go live with Aunt Martha (1).

3. Kapugen tells Julie that if she is unhappy she can marry Daniel (1) when she turns 13 years old (1). Kapugen promises to arrange everything with Daniel's father (1).

4. Yes, Julie does try to fit in with the Americanized Eskimos (1). She goes to school (1) and learns to read and write within a year (1). To learn more about their culture, she reads the encyclopedia in her free time (1). She cuts her hair and curls it so she'll look more like other Americans (1).

5. Judith corrects Julie and tells her it is called a charm bracelet (1). Then she and Rose laugh at Julie (1), causing her to blush with embarrassment (1). That night Julie throws away her own i'noGo tied because she wants very much to fit in with the other girls (1).

Passage #10: *Sounder*

1. A sheriff and two deputies (1) believe that the father stole a ham from a smokehouse (1), so they knock over a kitchen table (1) and handcuff him (1). When Sounder tries to get in the house, they say he's got to be held or they'll shoot him (1).

2. The deputy means that the father is going to be a prisoner (2), and prisoners wear black-and-white-striped outfits (1). He's saying that if the man tries to escape, he'll be an easy target to shoot (1).

3. When Sounder finally realizes that there are strangers in the house, he comes running from the field (1), barking loudly (1). When Sounder tries to get in the house, a deputy kicks both him and the boy off the porch (1). Then the deputy tells the boy to hold onto Sounder outdoors (1).

4. Sounder got loose because he was too big and strong for the boy to hold onto (1), especially when he lunged (1). Sounder chased after the wagon because the men were taking away his master (1), and he wanted to defend him (1).

5. The boy just saw the deputy turn around and shoot Sounder without any reason (1). Now he is afraid that the deputy may do the same thing to his father (1) if his father complains even a little bit (1).

Passage #11: *Roll of Thunder, Hear My Cry*

1. Cassie, her brothers, and their friends are black (1). The county provides a bus for white students to go to Jefferson Davis School (1), but does not provide a bus for the black students who attend Great Faith School (1). Therefore, the children have to walk to school every day because it is the only way to get there (1).

2. After it rains, the Jefferson Davis School bus driver always drives fast through the mud puddles to spray muddy water all over Cassie and the other children (1). Then one day the bus driver drives so recklessly that he almost runs over them (1), forcing them to jump into a ditch filled with dirty water (1).

3. Little Man feels angry and frustrated by the fact that the bus driver deliberately drives through the mud to spray Little Man's clothes with dirty water (1). He says it's unfair (1). He is humiliated and embarrassed, and he thinks the kids on the bus think that what the bus driver does to him is funny (1).

4. Big Ma accepts mistreatment as a fact of life (1) and would tell Little Man that since there's nothing he can do about it, he shouldn't worry (1). She would probably say to just take the book and use it (1).

5. The children start out for school early (1), hoping to avoid the bus. When they think they hear it coming, they climb up on an embankment (1), but it turns out to just be a car. Stacey urges them to stay on the high ground and wait until the bus goes by (1), but because it's raining hard, they decide to continue walking to school (1). The bus driver is driving very fast that morning (1) and acts like he's going to run over them with the bus (1). Since there's nowhere else for the children to go, they are forced to jump into a gully filled with muddy water (1).

Passage #12: *Tuck Everlasting*

1. The Tucks are unusual because they will live forever (1), and they cannot grow or change in any way (1).

2. No, Tuck doesn't enjoy being immortal at all (1)! He says that he feels stuck (1) and no longer a part of the wheel of life (1), like rocks beside the road. He wishes he could still grow and change (1), even though it means he would eventually die (1).

3. Tuck does not want the people in Treegap to know about the spring (1) that would make them unable to die (1). He thinks they'd trample each other to get to it (1) and, in the end, they would regret living forever (1).

4. Tuck says that life is like a wheel that is always turning (1) and never stopping (1). He tells Winnie that all creatures are born (1), live (1), and then die (1) to make room for the new ones.

5. She doesn't want to think about the fact that one day she will die (1) because she is afraid to die (1). She feels overwhelmed by what he's saying (1), and she's amazed that he's talking to her about such things (1).

Magazine Articles about Non-Living Things

Outline Student Guide

What's Important about a Non-Living Thing?

1. What is it?

   _____

2. What's been discovered about it?

   _____

   _____

3. How do you know? (facts/evidence)

   _____

   _____

   _____

4. What conclusions were drawn?

   _____

   _____

5. When did it happen?

   _____

6. Where did it happen?

   _____

7. Why did it happen?

   _____

   _____

8. Who made it happen?

   _____

9. Surprising/Interesting facts:

   _____

   _____

   _____

Magazine Articles About
Non-Living Things *(cont.)*
Graphic Organizer

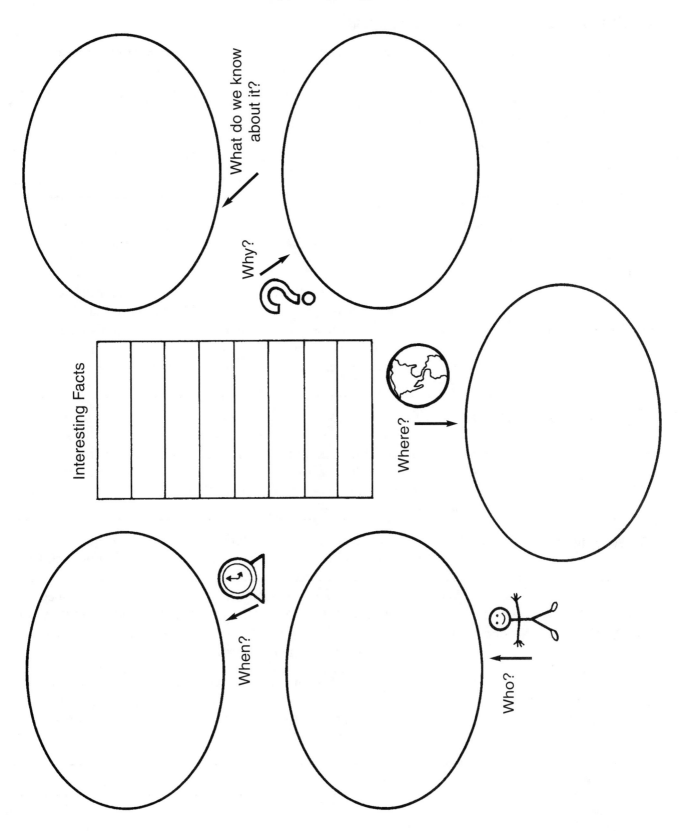

Magazine Articles about Non-Living Things (cont.)

Passage #1

Model the use of the outline on page 68 for this article.

Here are some words you will need to know as you listen to this magazine article:

suspension bridge: a bridge with a roadway that hangs in the air supported only by cables which are attached to towers

compressed air: air under great pressure

surpassed: went beyond

One of America's most famous bridges, the Brooklyn Bridge, took 14 years to build. It also took 21 lives and left its creator disabled for life. It spans the East River between the main part of New York City and Brooklyn.

After he had perfected a cable-weaving technique that made suspension bridges safer than ever before, John Roebling, a leading bridge expert, finally got permission to build the longest suspension bridge ever. Suspension bridges had failed in many places due to high winds. But with his idea of cable stays running up diagonally from stone towers, it was finally safe to have a roadway hang from gigantic cables supported by two huge towers standing on the bedrock under the river.

In 1869 John Roebling caught tetanus while surveying the site for the bridge and died just a few weeks later. His son, Washington Roebling, did not want his father's dream to die and so took over leadership of the project. However, it was his wife Emily who would finish it. In June of 1872, Washington developed a serious illness caused by working for too many hours in the compressed air atmosphere under the East River. He refused to follow his doctor's orders to rest; and in December of 1872 he collapsed. He never returned to the bridge again but continuously watched its progress through binoculars from his bedroom window.

When he finally accepted that he was permanently disabled, Roebling sent Emily as his representative—although at that time no woman had ever before worked on a construction project, let alone directed it. At first, the workers refused to take orders from Emily, but her thorough understanding of the bridge and knowledge of construction helped her to gradually win their respect; and they eventually accepted her as their new leader. Roebling had days when he couldn't get up from his bed and other days when he couldn't speak, but he designed a way to tap messages into his wife's palm. She would then carry these instructions to the construction supervisors.

The Brooklyn Bridge opened in May of 1883 with a huge celebration. It still stands today, and it carries a far greater amount of daily traffic than was ever anticipated. Fortunately, Roebling had the bridge constructed to standards that far surpassed those of the nineteenth century, insisting on making it six times stronger than necessary.

Magazine Articles About Non-Living Things (cont.)

Passage #1 Questions

1. Where is the Brooklyn Bridge? Why was it built? (*3 points*)

   _____

   _____

   _____

2. What makes the Brooklyn Bridge a suspension bridge? How was it built? (*3 points*)

   _____

   _____

3. Outline the series of events that took the leadership of the Brooklyn Bridge away from the creator of the bridge to the person who oversaw its last stages of construction. (*6 points*)

   _____

   _____

   _____

   _____

   _____

   _____

4. What were the problems Washington Roebling had as a result of working in the compressed air for too long? (*4 points*)

   _____

   _____

   _____

5. Explain why you agree or disagree with this statement:

   The workers didn't want to take orders from Emily Roebling. (*4 points*)

   _____

   _____

   _____

Magazine Articles about
Non-Living Things (cont.)

Passage #2

Use the outline on page 68 for this article.

Here are some words that you will need to know as you listen to this magazine article:

immigrant: a person who comes to live in a country other than his native one
consistent: the same; stable
rivets: a type of metal bolt used to hold two things together
patent: a legal document giving only the inventor the right to make, use, and sell his/her invention for a set period of time

---

Denim blue jeans are recognized worldwide as classic American pants. Americans spend billions of dollars every year on jeans, and practically every person in America owns a pair.

Jeans came about more than 150 years ago as a result of the gold rush. In 1849 the California Gold Rush attracted tens of thousands of gold prospectors to the San Francisco area. Nineteen-year-old Levi Strauss, a recent Jewish immigrant from Germany, left his home in Louisville, Kentucky, in order to start a store to supply goods for these gold miners. He boarded a ship in New York City and spent a very long journey sailing around Cape Horn at the tip of South America to reach the West Coast. Through his conversations with the prospectors, Levi found that what the men really wanted most was a durable pair of pants that could endure the stresses of digging and mining. During his voyage, Levi also sold cloth to his fellow passengers. By the time the boat docked in San Francisco, he had only a few rolls of canvas left. Recognizing the ready market for sturdy pants, he immediately hired a tailor to sew trousers from his remaining rolls of brown canvas. These pants sold rapidly, and word spread quickly about their quality.

Because the demand for the pants grew so fast, the brown canvas soon ran out. Levi searched for another fabric and decided to try "serge de Nimes," a heavy cotton cloth created in Nimes, France. He shortened the name to denim and chose to dye the material a dark indigo blue since it gave the most consistent color. People began calling the pants "blue denims" or "blue jeans." The word "jeans" actually resulted from the mispronunciation of Genoa, Italy, the name of the town that manufactured the fabric for Levi.

A further improvement to the design of the jeans came during the 1860s when a miner named Alkali Ike stuffed his pockets with so much gold ore that they repeatedly tore open. He took his torn pants to tailor Jake Davis. Frustrated because his mending didn't last, Jake decided to take Ike's pants to the local blacksmith and have copper rivets attached to the pocket corners. Ike's jeans stopped tearing, and Jake found he suddenly had many other clients who wanted their pants pockets riveted, too. Jake presented his idea to Levi, and they became partners in a patent for Levi's jeans with riveted pockets.

Today's Levis bear a great resemblance to the originals. They even bear the original trademark of two horses trying to pull apart a pair of his jeans. Levi's good idea turned into a booming business, and now people worldwide purchase more than 425 million pairs of jeans annually.

Magazine Articles about
Non-Living Things *(cont.)*
Passage #2 Questions

1. When were denim jeans invented, who invented them, and why did he do it? *(3 points)*

_____

_____

_____

_____

2. Who was Jake Davis, and what role did he play in the improvement of jeans? *(5 points)*

_____

_____

_____

3. How did the name "jeans" come about? *(3 points)*

_____

_____

_____

4. What made jeans immediately popular? *(3 points)*

_____

_____

_____

5. Tell what you know about denim jeans today. *(6 points)*

_____

_____

_____

_____

_____

_____

Magazine Articles about Non-Living Things *(cont.)*

Passage #3

Model the use of the graphic organizer on page 69 for this article.

Here are some words that you will need to know as you listen to this magazine article:

penetrates: enters into
refined: perfected
Surgeon General: the head doctor for the U.S. government

In September of 1928, a spore flew in the open window of a London hospital and landed in a culture dish of bacteria. Alexander Fleming, the researcher growing the bacteria for study, noticed a green mold spreading throughout the dish. It appeared to dissolve the bacteria!

Fleming, horrified by the number of soldiers with infected wounds he saw die in World War I, had devoted his life to finding something to fight bacteria. He had just discovered penicillin. However, many years passed before penicillin was used in the fight against disease. To determine if it was toxic, Fleming first tested it on white mice and rabbits, then later on his lab assistant, Stuart Craddock, who willingly ate some of the mold without suffering any ill effects.

Penicillin works because germs are living cells. Penicillin penetrates the germ cell wall and causes the cell matter to flow out of it, thus killing the cell. Doctors called penicillin an antibiotic, which means "against a way of life"—germ life!

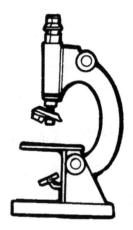

Oxford University researchers Dr. Ernst Chain and Professor Howard Florey, excited by Fleming's research findings, refined the drug for use in humans. Yet, when World War II broke out, even though thousands of their soldiers were again dying of infected wounds, Great Britain refused to act. So Chain and Florey turned to America. America immediately saw the incredible possibilities for penicillin and made massive amounts for use with the military. Due to these efforts, by the end of the war almost 95 percent of Allied troops with infected wounds recovered.

However, penicillin was used only for military personnel. Late in the summer of 1943, a two-year-old girl in New York City was dying from blood poisoning. Her desperate father begged a newspaper editor to intervene on her behalf. The editor contacted the U.S. Surgeon General, who in turned called the only doctor in the country with permission to release penicillin for civilian use. He agreed, and the little girl's doctor drove hundreds of miles with a police escort to obtain the precious medicine. The child received her first dose just an hour and a half before doctors expected her to die. She recovered, and today antibiotics such as penicillin are used routinely on bacterial infections.

Magazine Articles about
Non-Living Things *(cont.)*

Passage #3 Questions

1. What was the first antibiotic? Who discovered it? When and how was it discovered? (*5 points*)

_____

_____

_____

_____

2. How does penicillin work? (*4 points*)

_____

_____

_____

3. What three types of living beings tested the new drug to determine its safety? (*4 points*)

_____

_____

_____

4. Who convinced the United States to produce penicillin and for what purpose? (*4 points*)

_____

_____

_____

5. Why was it significant that the dying child received the miracle drug? (*3 points*)

_____

_____

_____

Magazine Articles about Non-Living Things *(cont.)*

Passage #4

Use the graphic organizer on page 69 for this article.

Here are some words that you will need to know as you listen to this magazine article:

missile site: location from which missles are launched
transmit: to send
relay: to pass along

A satellite is any object in space travelling a regular path, or orbit, around another object. For example, Earth is a satellite of the sun, and the moon is a satellite that orbits the Earth. In 1957 the Russians launched *Sputnik*, the first artificial satellite. Today 5,000 artificial satellites orbit our planet. These satellites take measurements, observe things happening on Earth, and help communications.

Multistage rockets boost artificial satellites into orbit. Each rocket stage fires in turn, then falls away after depleting its fuel, until just the satellite remains. Since an orbit must match the pull of Earth's gravity to hold the satellite in place, each satellite must be placed at an exact height and speed. Satellites closest to Earth must move much faster than those farther away. Although satellites look different externally, they all carry instruments to take measurements, computers to store data, control units to perform instructions from Earth, and communications units to send information back to Earth. Because no night or clouds exist in space, the sun always shines, allowing satellites to use solar cell power. The solar cells collect the sun's rays and change them into electricity. They can work for years without needing repair or replacement. All satellites have cameras and computers to record, analyze, and store data until they send it to Earth. Depending on their function, most satellites also have sensors to recognize light, color, heat, water, minerals, and gases.

Six different types of satellites orbit at varying heights above our planet's surface. Environmental satellites stay close to watch oceans, icebergs, volcanoes, deserts, forests fires, and moving animal herds such as whales. They also measure pollution in the atmosphere and holes in the ozone layer. Military, or spy, satellites watch missile sites and the movement of armies and navies. Weather satellites record cloud movements and wind speeds. Navigational satellites let sea and land vehicles know their precise location on the Earth's surface. Astronomical satellites keep track of stars, comets, and meteors. Communications satellites stay in fixed orbits, which means they travel so high above the Earth that they always stay directly above the equator. They relay telephone, television, and radio signals. Using antennae, they pick up the signals for sound, pictures, and voices from Earth and transmit them to another part of the world.

Communications satellites enable you to see things as they happen in faraway places. Trucks with mobile units travel to wherever news is happening. They record the scene with a camera which transmits, or uplinks, it to a satellite. The satellite then downlinks, or sends it back, to earth stations worldwide. Earth stations, also called satellite dishes, then transmit these signals to your television set.

Magazine Articles about
Non-Living Things *(cont.)*
Passage #4 Questions

1. Name two natural satellites and what they orbit around. (*2 points*)

   _____

   _____

   _____

2. List at least four of the things that all artificial satellites have on board. (*4 points*)

   _____

   _____

   _____

   _____

3. Explain how an artificial satellite gets into orbit. (*3 points*)

   _____

   _____

   _____

   _____

4. Why is a specific orbit necessary for each satellite? (*3 points*)

   _____

   _____

   _____

5. Name and explain the purpose of four of the different kinds of artificial satellites that orbit our planet. (*8 points*)

   _____

   _____

   _____

   _____

   _____

   _____

Magazine Articles about
Non-Living Things *(cont.)*

Passage #5

Do not use student guide pages for this article.

Here is a word that you will need to know as you listen to this magazine article:

ozone: a poisonous, blue, gaseous form of oxygen

Lightning, one of nature's most powerful forces, can destroy buildings and trees, kill people and animals, and start raging fires. Most often we associate it with thunderstorms. Yet lightning can also occur during snowstorms, sandstorms, tornadoes, and even in the smoke and ashes released by an erupting volcano.

Lightning occurs to restore the natural electrical balance in clouds. Everything has extremely tiny negatively charged particles called electrons. Lightning happens when electrons at the bottom of a thunder cloud are pulled toward the positively charged particles at the top of the cloud. In the resulting burst of heat and light, a stream of electrons moves within a cloud or between clouds at a speed of almost 270,000 miles per hour (434,430 kph). As the electrons jump, they heat the air so much that it glows. Lightning looks jagged because electrons follow the wettest path. Scientists call this jagged appearance a stepped ladder. This most dangerous type of lightning occurs when a positive electrical charge builds up on the ground, causing the electrons in the cloud to race toward the Earth. As the stepped ladder gets closer to Earth's surface, a stream of positively charged particles flows up from the ground to greet it. Usually this kind of lightning strikes the tallest object in an area; in fact, the Empire State Building in New York City receives an average of 23 lightning strikes per year! When lightning strikes a beach, it instantly melts the sand into a type of glass called fulgurite.

A thunderclap follows every lightning flash. The sudden heat of the lightning makes moist air explode outward, causing the sound waves we call thunder. People call silent lightning storms that look like lights flashing on and off in the clouds heat lightning, but actually they just can't hear the thunder because it's 15 (24 km) or more miles away.

Scientists don't know what causes ball lightning, the rarest form of lightning. It resembles a glowing melon-sized ball floating through the air or rolling along the ground. Ball lightning can travel up or down or even come through a window.

Every second, approximately 100 lightning bolts strike in various places on Earth. Lightning strikes some parts of the Earth more often than others; the equator, due to its concentration of warm, moist air, receives strikes most frequently. Lightning hits large airplanes about once every two years, but fortunately the plane can usually keep flying.

A lightning bolt's heat exceeds the temperature on the surface of the sun and ranges in length from 9 feet (3 m) long to over 90 miles (145 km). Yet, since every bolt produces ozone gas—which protects us from the radiation of the sun—lightning helps our planet. It also cleans the air by causing pollution particles to fall to the ground.

Magazine Articles about
Non-Living Things (cont.)

Passage #5 Questions

1. Why are many people so afraid of lightning? How hot is a lightning bolt? (*5 points*)

_____

_____

_____

_____

2. What are the benefits of lightning? (*4 points*)

_____

_____

_____

3. In addition to thunderstorms, under what other conditions can lightning occur? (*4 points*)

_____

_____

_____

4. What is the relationship between thunder and lightning? (*3 points*)

_____

_____

_____

5. Explain why you agree or disagree with this statement:

   Lightning does not strike the same place twice. (*4 points*)

_____

_____

_____

_____

Magazine Articles about Non-Living Things *(cont.)*

Passage #6

Do not use student guide pages for this article.

> Here are some words that you will need to know as you listen to this magazine article:
>
> **crystallize:** to change into crystals
> **minute:** tiny
> **adorn:** decorate
> **synthetic:** manmade

Diamonds, the hardest naturally occurring mineral, are also the most valuable gemstones. They form in the Earth's mantle, where intense temperature and high pressure cause carbon to crystallize. Over thousands of years, these diamonds move closer to the Earth's surface as the result of earthquakes and volcanic eruptions. Named for the Greek word *adamas*, which means "unconquerable," a diamond can only be cut by another diamond. However, a sharp, accurate blow will split a diamond because of its cleavage, or ability to split along lines. A diamond will not dissolve in acid, but it can be destroyed by extreme heat.

In 1867 a child who found a pretty pebble on the banks of the Orange River in South Africa actually discovered the world's largest diamond mine. Most of the world's gem-quality diamonds come from South Africa. In 1979 huge deposits of diamonds were also discovered in western Australia. Diamonds cost a lot of money because even in the richest deposits, more than a ton of rock must be dug up and crushed to produce one small diamond. In fact, some mines produce only one carat of diamonds for every 6,000 pounds of rock mined. The largest natural diamond ever found weighed 3,106 carats prior to cutting. Named the Cullinan, it was found in South Africa in 1905.

Gem diamonds are graded according to their weight, cut, clarity, and color. The larger the carats, or weight, the more valuable. An outstanding cut is crucial, for diamonds have an unequalled ability to reflect and refract rays of light, a quality that is further enhanced when many facets, or sides, are cut and polished on the stone. Each tiny facet must be exactly the correct size, shape, and angle in relation to the other facets to get the right effect. Almost all diamonds today have the brilliant cut of 58 facets.

Clarity ratings include flaws such as inclusions (tiny air bubbles) or minute cracks called fissures. Most stones have a yellowish tint, but the most valuable diamonds have no color. Besides white, diamonds also come in yellow, pink, blue, black, brown, green, purple, and the rarest color, red. In Europe, America, and Japan, diamonds adorn many engagement and wedding rings.

About half of the world's natural diamonds are suitable only for industrial use. Manufacturers need diamonds to cut, grind, and shape with great accuracy the hard materials used in the production of cars, planes, and engines. Mining drill bits need diamond tips. The industrial demand for diamonds cannot be met by natural diamonds, so General Electric Research Laboratories created the first synthetic diamond in 1954 by compressing carbon under extremely high heat and pressure. These synthetic diamonds cost much more than natural ones, and therefore they are not used in jewelry.

Magazine Articles about Non-Living Things (cont.)

Passage #6 Questions

1. How do diamonds form? How do they get in the Earth's crust? (*4 points*)

_____

_____

_____

_____

2. When and where were the world's two largest diamond mines found? (*4 points*)

_____

_____

_____

3. What are some uses for diamonds? (*3 points*)

_____

_____

_____

4. Define facets and why they are so important to diamonds. (*5 points*)

_____

_____

_____

_____

_____

5. Name four of the unusual colors found in rare diamonds. (*4 points*)

_____

_____

_____

Magazine Articles about Living Things
Outline Student Guide

What's Important about a Living Thing (Plant or Animal)?

1. Name: _____

   Type (fungus, tree, mammal, bird, etc): _____

2. Where does it live? _____

   _____

3. How long does it live? _____

4. What does it look like? Unique characteristics: _____

   _____

   _____

5. How does it get food? _____

   _____

6. How does it reproduce? _____

   _____

7. Who or what are its enemies? _____

   _____

8. Is it endangered? If yes, why? _____

   _____

   _____

9. Why is it important to humans? _____

   _____

   _____

   _____

Magazine Articles about
Living Things *(cont.)*

Graphic Organizer

What's Important about a Living Thing (Plant or Animal)?

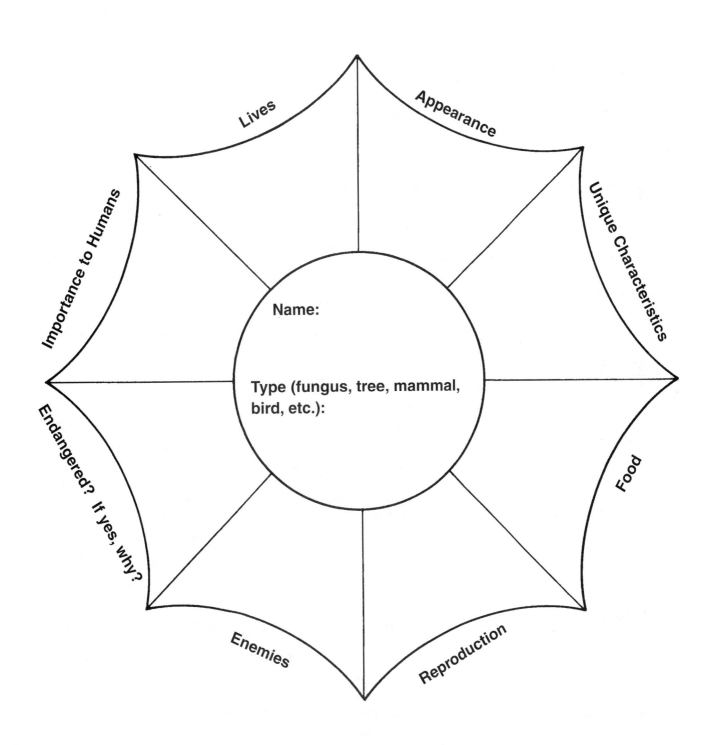

Magazine Articles about Living Things *(cont.)*

Passage #7

Model the use of the outline on page 82 for this article.

Here are some words that you will need to know as you listen to this magazine article:

perish: die
century: one hundred years
durability: capability of lasting a very long time
conservationists: people who are concerned with the welfare of plants and wildlife

Many people know that California's state tree, the redwood, grows taller than any other living thing on our planet. In fact, the tallest one ever found measured an astonishing 385 feet (117 m)—the height of a 38-story skyscraper. Fossils prove that redwoods existed 130 million years ago, and mounting evidence indicates that these impressive trees have actually inhabited our Earth for 200 million years. Since they require a foggy climate that gets neither too hot nor too cold, they have a very limited growing area, which stretches from Big Sur, California, to the southern border of Oregon. Upon first encountering a redwood, it often shocks people that they usually have no branches for their first 150 feet (46 m) above the ground. Yet these same gigantic trees produce short, stubby, flat needles and tiny pine cones less than an inch long.

Another well-known fact about redwoods is that they can live for thousands of years—longer than any other living thing on Earth. So far, the oldest redwood ever cut down was about 2,200 years old, but many scientists believe redwoods can live for 4,000 years. It appears that their only enemies are windstorms and chainsaws. With their deeply grooved bark up to one foot thick (30 cm), these ancient conifers are immune to disease, parasites, insect attacks, fungi, and even forest fires. Although their bark may burn, the core of the tree will survive, refusing to perish even when subjected to intense heat up to 3000° F (1649° C). Damage caused by such a fire can take more than a century to heal, but that is a short time given their lifespan. Due to their incredible height, lightning often strikes them and can cause some serious injury, but they always heal. Even those blown down by high winds refuse to die; if the severed roots of a fallen tree remain in the ground, dozens of new saplings will arise and grow at a pace of eight to twelve inches (20–30 cm) per year. A cut stump or broken-off trunk will also send up sprouts. These massive trees are so hardy that none have been known to die due to old age.

Redwood bark ranges in color from red to cinnamon brown, but the wood is always a clear light red that doesn't rot when exposed to weather but instead turns an attractive dark red. This makes them very desirable as a building material. During the California Gold Rush in the 1850s, many homes needed to be built quickly. People began cutting down the redwoods because their timber cannot fall susceptible to termites and has an extraordinary resistance to fire. Their wood's amazing durability and the fact that a single tree can provide as much as half a million board feet of lumber makes them extremely valuable to the lumber industry. As a result, 95 percent of the original trees have disappeared, and most of the remaining redwoods stand on land owned by lumber companies. However, conservationists have managed to get 70,000 acres (28,329 hectares) of redwood forest preserved as public parks.

Magazine Articles about Living Things *(cont.)*

Passage #7 Questions

1. What two facts do many people know about the amazing redwood tree? *(2 points)*

   _____

   _____

2. What qualities do redwood trees have that make them such desirable lumber? *(5 points)*

   _____

   _____

   _____

3. What happens to redwood trees that are caught in a forest fire? *(3 points)*

   _____

   _____

   _____

4. Why are conservationists concerned about the redwood trees, and what have they done about it? *(3 points)*

   _____

   _____

   _____

   _____

5. Explain why you agree or disagree with this statement:

   Redwood trees are very hardy. *(7 points)*

   _____

   _____

   _____

   _____

   _____

Magazine Articles about Living Things (cont.)

Passage #8

Use the outline on page 82 for this article.

Here are some words that you will need to know as you listen to this magazine article:

crevice: deep crack
voles: mouse-like animals with stubby tails
pesticides: chemicals used to kill harmful insects

Flying over plains, swamps, farm fields, and even deserts, barn owls live on every continent except Antarctica. Barn owls received their name because long ago farmers built small openings called "owl windows" high under the roof gables of barns. They welcomed the owls because they ate the rats and mice that ate grain.

With their keen sense of hearing, eyes that pierce the darkness, and strong talons, barn owls make excellent nighttime predators. In flight, their wingspan of 44 inches (112 cm) dwarfs their tiny one-pound (0.45-kg), 18-inch (46-cm) long bodies. Barn owls communicate with bloodcurdling screeches, using one call to defend their hunting territory and another to attract a mate. Still, their most outstanding characteristic is their white, heart-shaped faces.

After winter ends, a male barn owl begins the courtship ritual. He swoops out of the darkness to grab an unsuspecting mouse with his viselike claws. Then he brings the mouse to a female. Once she accepts him, they search for a nesting site such as a barn or abandoned building, a rock crevice, or a large hole in a tree.

The barn owls mate in late spring. Over the course of the next ten days, the female lays three to eleven eggs. She sits on the eggs, getting up only to use her face and beak to turn them to insure even heating. The male brings her all her food during the four weeks she stays with the eggs.

Finally, muffled sounds come from within the eggs. Slowly, the blind, naked owlets use the special bump on top of their beaks—called an egg tooth—to break out of the eggs. After 10 days, the babies can see and their tiny bodies grow fluffy white down. Their mother feeds them tiny scraps torn from prey delivered by the father. Soon both parents must begin hunting before dusk until after dawn to get all the food necessary to satisfy their babies' growing appetites.

When the owlets' speckled feathers appear, both parents leave the nest and roost elsewhere, returning only to bring food. After eight to ten weeks the owlets fly from the nest. During years when prey such as voles, frogs, birds, rats, chipmunks, and other small animals are plentiful, the parents may then lay another set of eggs.

If they can survive their first year, barn owls can live up to 30 years. Unfortunately, half of all owlets starve within a year of leaving their nest. Barn owls' only natural enemies are the goshawk and humans. However, many die after being hit by cars or electrocuted by electrical wires. Since today there are fewer barns and old buildings for nesting as well as an increasing use of pesticides, barn owls, though once plentiful, are now endangered. As a result, Congress has made it illegal to shoot any owl in America, and conservationists provide nesting boxes.

Magazine Articles about Living Things (cont.)

Passage #8 Questions

1. How did barn owls receive their name? (*2 points*)

   _____

   _____

2. Describe five physical characteristics of barn owls. (*5 points*)

   _____

   _____

   _____

   _____

   _____

3. Name three of the barn owl's favorite things to eat. (*3 points*)

   _____

   _____

   _____

4. What happens after a pair of barn owls find a nesting site? (*6 points*)

   _____

   _____

   _____

   _____

5. Name four of the main causes of death for the barn owl. (*4 points*)

   _____

   _____

   _____

   _____

Magazine Articles about Living Things *(cont.)*

Passage #9

Model the use of the graphic organizer on page 83 for this article.

Here are some words that you will need to know as you listen to this magazine article:

strewn: scattered
cultivated: taken care of by a person
consumption: amount eaten

The first time in written history that strawberries were mentioned, they had a different name. Thousands of years ago someone named them "strewberries" because their fruit appears to be strewn all over the plant. Over time, people started calling them strawberries. Today, strawberries—those tasty, heart-shaped fruits so many of us love to eat—grow in almost every country in the world.

In spring, existing strawberry plants grow new leaves. Then they put more roots into the earth to get more water and nutrients. As the days lengthen, the plant's leaves spread out to get the maximum possible sunlight.

Next, the strawberry plant produces flower buds covered by tiny green leaves. When these buds open, their flowers consist of a group of small yellow stalks covered with pollen dust and surrounded by five white petals. These flowers need pollination to grow into strawberries. Fortunately, as bees visit the flowers, some of the pollen sticks to their bodies. When a bee moves to another plant, it transfers this pollen.

Each pollinated flower turns into a strawberry. First, the petals drop off, leaving just the middle section, which begins to swell. Next, very tiny seeds form on the strawberry's outer skin. As it grows and enlarges, these seeds spread farther apart. Each tiny seed has a vein joining it to the center of the strawberry for nourishment.

At first the little strawberry is green, but as it grows, it turns to creamy white, then pink, and finally red. Then people, birds, and small animals such as mice and moles feast on the ripe strawberries. Some of the strawberries fall to the ground, allowing the seeds to reach the soil and begin a new plant.

However, the majority of strawberry plants do not get started this way! A strawberry has two ways to reproduce. As the strawberries grow, long creeping stems also begin growing along the ground. These stems, called runners, can reach several feet in length. Each strawberry plant sends out up to a dozen runners, and each one grows into a new plant. The tip of each runner has a bud protected by tiny hairs. Eventually, this bud opens, and three small leaves begin to unfold. The tiny new plant puts roots into the ground, but the runner continues to carry nutrition to it from the parent plant until autumn. By then, the young plant begun by the runner can survive by itself. The plants rest during the winter and awaken in the spring. A strawberry plant will repeat this cycle for up to six years.

Each year, California produces 75 percent of all strawberries eaten in the United States. A recent survey based on consumption rated the strawberry as the fourth most popular fruit in America. Their popularity may be due to the fact that they provide vitamin C, protein, and fiber with few calories and almost no fat. Or maybe it's just because they taste so good!

Magazine Articles about Living Things *(cont.)*

Passage #9 Questions

1. Tell what strawberry plants do in the spring to prepare themselves to produce buds. (*3 points*)

   _____

   _____

   _____

2. Explain how a strawberry blossom turns into a strawberry that you can eat. (*5 points*)

   _____

   _____

   _____

   _____

   _____

3. Describe the two different ways strawberry plants reproduce. (*5 points*)

   _____

   _____

   _____

   _____

   _____

4. Name four of the reasons why strawberries are such a popular fruit in America. (*4 points*)

   _____

   _____

   _____

   _____

5. Explain why you agree or disagree with this statement:

   Each year California grows all the strawberries eaten in the world. (*3 points*)

   _____

   _____

   _____

   _____

Magazine Articles about Living Things *(cont.)*

Passage #10

Use the graphic organizer on page 83 for this article.

Here are some words that you will need to know as you listen to this magazine article:

sultan: ruler
consume: eat
convicts: people judged guilty of a crime
descendants: offspring (You are descendants of your parents and grandparents, etc.)

One of the world's scariest creatures, the komodo dragon, lives on Komodo Island in Indonesia, which is located between Australia and Southeast Asia. The source of ancient Asian dragon myths, komodo dragons are the largest lizards in the world, often growing to more than 10 feet (3 m) long and weighing up to 300 pounds (136 kg). The thick scales on their bodies resemble a knight's armor, and their forked tongues flick in and out constantly as they smell for possible prey.

In addition to their terrifying appearance, komodo dragons have extremely bad breath caused by the bacteria in rotten meat. Unlike most animals, dragons actually prefer decaying meat to fresh. Dragons can run up to 10 miles an hour (16 kph) for short distances and have the ability to unhinge their jaws to swallow pieces of meat larger than their own heads. Extremely skilled at hunting, they track an animal silently, then charge it, making a noise like a machine gun. Their claws alone equal the length of a human adult's longest fingers, and their razor-sharp teeth have curved, jagged edges to keep their victims from escaping. In the unlikely event a victim does escape, it won't live anyway, since the infection caused by the bacteria in the dragon's mouth kills within three days. Dragons generally eat deer, wild pigs, livestock, and water buffalo, but they will consume any human they can catch.

Komodo dragons dig deep burrows in which to live. When mating time comes, the male must bring a large gift, such as a pig's head, before the female will accept him. She then buries between 10 and 30 eggs deep under the ground where the temperature remains constant. After eight months, the baby dragons hatch and dig themselves out of the nest. They receive no care from their parents; in fact, their parents will eat them! So the babies hide in treetops to avoid capture by adult dragons and only sneak down to clean up the scraps left when all the adults have finished eating a kill.

Long ago, the Sultan of Bima sent convicts to the island to meet their fate at the claws of the dragons. The prisoners' descendants still live on the island, although the dragons outnumber the people on the island two to one. People must build their houses on stilts to avoid dragon attacks and place boulders on the graves of their deceased relatives to prevent the dragons from digging them up to eat.

Since they occupy the top spot in the food chain, only occasional volcanic eruptions, tidal waves caused by these eruptions, and larger members of their own species pose natural threats to the komodo dragon. Yet today the dragon is an endangered species because its major sources of prey have been hunted too widely by humans. Therefore, the Indonesian government protects them and has declared their island a national park.

Magazine Articles about Living Things (cont.)

Passage #10 Questions

1. Explain six features that make komodo dragons look so frightening. (*6 points*)

_____

_____

_____

_____

_____

2. How do komodo dragons locate and capture prey? What happens when the prey escapes? (*5 points*)

_____

_____

_____

_____

_____

3. What must baby komodo dragons do to stay alive? Why? (*3 points*)

_____

_____

_____

4. What makes life difficult for the people who live near the komodo dragons? (*3 points*)

_____

_____

_____

5. Explain why you agree or disagree with this statement:
Komodo dragons live only on several islands near Asia. (*3 points*)

_____

_____

_____

Magazine Articles about Living Things (cont.)

Passage #11

Do not use student guide pages for this article.

Here is a word that you will need to know as you listen to this magazine article:

sieve: strainer

Each year most Americans consume about 100 pounds (45 kg) of wheat products. Wheat products include any foods made with flour such as bread, cereal, pancakes, muffins, waffles, cakes, pie crusts, donuts, pretzels, crackers, dinner rolls, cookies, noodles, and macaroni.

Wheat belongs to the grass family. A grain of wheat consists of three parts: the bran (the kernel's outer covering), the wheat germ (which can grow into a new plant), and the endosperm. White flour comes from ground-up endosperm. Whole wheat flour, made from the entire wheat kernel, has more B vitamins, fiber, protein, and minerals than white flour.

Before they plant the wheat with a grain drill, farmers work their soil to break up clumps of dirt and kill weeds. The grain drill performs four tasks: its blade cuts a trench in the soil for the seeds; a tube right behind this blade drops one seed at a time; another tube squirts some fertilizer; and a wheel presses soil over the seeds.

The seed sends out tiny roots, then a shoot that pokes up through the soil. Then it grows leaves, which store nourishment. Next, the plant sends up its spikes. Stored nutrients from the leaves flow up these spikes, which can reach two to four feet (0.6–1.2 m) high. At the top of each spike grows a head containing 20–50 wheat kernels. Once these kernels ripen, the wheat turns golden and dries out. The drier the grain the better, for moist kernels can become moldy and spoil in storage.

Now the farmer harvests the wheat using a combine, a machine which cuts the wheat, separates the grain from the husk and straw, and stores the grain in a tank. This tank gets emptied into a truck, which takes it to a grain elevator for storage. Inside grain elevators, wheat can keep for many months without spoiling.

When the wheat leaves these elevators, it travels to a mill where it goes through a seven-step process. First the grains run through sorting disks to eliminate dirt, then past a magnet to remove metal pieces. Next, it's washed in a special tub designed so that the wheat floats to the top while heavier things fall to the bottom. In the next step, the grains pass between heavy rollers that break them into little pieces. These pieces pass through sorting screens. This process repeats until the bran separates from the kernels, gets blown away by fans, and collects separately. Finally, rollers crush the remaining tiny bits of endosperm into flour. In the last step just before packaging, the flour flows through a fine sieve. The bran and germ gets sold as animal feed or used in whole-wheat products, such as breads, cereals, or muffins.

People in the Middle East began growing wheat almost 10,000 years ago. Today, wheat gives more nourishment to more people than any other food. Since it can grow anywhere except the polar regions and the tropics, each month of the year wheat is harvested somewhere in the world.

Magazine Articles about Living Things (cont.)

Passage #11 Questions

1. Why is wheat such an important grain? (*4 points*)

_____

_____

_____

_____

2. Explain the life cycle of a wheat plant from seed to harvest. (*5 points*)

_____

_____

_____

_____

3. What happens to the wheat grain after it has been harvested? (*4 points*)

_____

_____

_____

4. Describe the 7-step process wheat goes through once it reaches the mill. (*7 points*)

_____

_____

_____

_____

_____

_____

_____

Magazine Articles about Living Things *(cont.)*

Passage #12

Do not use student guide pages for this article.

Here is a term that you will need to know as you listen to this magazine article:

coral reef: an ocean mound consisting of the bodies of tiny sea animals called coral

What has a monkey-like tail, a horse-like head, a kangaroo-like pouch, an insect-like skeleton, and eyes that move separately like a chameleon's? It's the small, peculiar fish called a sea horse. Sea horses, named for their resemblance to horses, have long, flexible tails capable of grasping, and they use them to cling to sea plants. In addition to their internal skeletons, they have external skeletons made of bony plates. They eat microscopic sea creatures called plankton by sucking them up their long snouts like a vacuum cleaner.

A sea horse cannot swim well because it must rely on a tiny dorsal fin on its back to move through the water in an upright position. This dorsal fin moves more than 2,000 times a minute. To stay afloat at the correct depth, sea horses have an internal organ called a swim bladder.

Sea horses reproduce in an extremely unusual way. The male has a pouch into which the female lays up to one hundred eggs. The male carries these eggs in his pouch for six weeks. Then he labors for up to two days to give birth to tiny, live babies, each a mere ¼ inch (0.6 cm) long. To keep from being swept away by ocean currents immediately after birth, the baby sea horses instinctively form small schools by holding tails as they travel. When they reach a safe patch of seaweed or a coral reef, they release their hold on one another and go their separate ways.

If they avoid predators, sea horses can live up to three years. Many animals that try to eat a sea horse will spit it out because of the bony knobs and spines that cover its body. To hide from the dogfish, sharks, eels, barracudas, stingrays, and sea turtles that will eat them anyway, sea horses cling to coral reefs and use camouflage coloring. This means they can change to almost any color so that they blend in with their background and become almost unnoticeable. In addition, when a sea horse gets frightened, it curls its tail around its snout and makes itself as small as possible.

About 25 different species of sea horses exist. Small sea horses live in shallow tropical waters off the Florida coast, in the Gulf of Mexico, and in the Caribbean Sea. Larger sea horses live off the coasts of California, Australia, and New Zealand. The smallest adult sea horse ever found measured just an inch and a half (4 cm) while the largest known sea horse measured 14 inches (36 cm) in length.

Sea horses have become very popular in saltwater aquariums, since they thrive in an artificial environment and can actually be tamed. Over time, when a person reaches in to put food into their aquarium, they will rush over. Some will wrap their tails around a finger and others may allow themselves to be gently petted on the head.

Magazine Articles about
Living Things (cont.)

Passage #12 Questions

1. List five of the many interesting physical characteristics of the sea horse. (*5 points*)

_____

_____

_____

_____

_____

2. Explain the unusual reproduction process of the sea horse. (*3 points*)

_____

_____

_____

_____

3. Where are sea horses found? Does where they live make a difference in their size?
   (*4 points*)

_____

_____

_____

_____

4. Name four enemies of the sea horse. (*4 points*)

_____

_____

_____

_____

5. Why might a person buy a sea horse for his/her aquarium? (*4 points*)

_____

_____

_____

_____

Magazine Articles

Use this scoring guide in conjunction with the answer key to assess student performance.

Scoring Guide			
Points Possible	**Exemplary Score**	**Average Score**	**Minimum Passing Score**
20	17–20	14–16	12

Answer Key

Passage #1: Brooklyn Bridge

1. The bridge is in New York (1). It was built to allow people and vehicles to cross the East River (1). The bridge connects New York City and Brooklyn (1).

2. The Brooklyn Bridge is a suspension bridge because it has a roadway hanging from huge cables (1). These cables are attached to towers (1) that are standing on the bedrock (1) under the river.

3. John Roebling designed the bridge (1), but he died before contruction began (1). His son, Washington, took over (1), but he became disabled while working on the bridge (1). He sent his wife, Emily, to oversee completion of the bridge (1); she did (1).

4. The illness made Washington collapse (1), and he couldn't return to work (1). Some days he couldn't get out of bed (1); other days, he couldn't speak (1).

5. I agree (1). They at first refused to take orders from a woman (1). They objected because no woman had ever directed a construction project (1) or even worked at a construction site. Eventually her leadership was accepted (1). **OR** I disagree (1). Though they initially rejected her (1), they slowly came to respect Emily's knowledge of the bridge and its construction (1). They accepted her as a leader (1).

Passage #2: Levi Jeans

1. They were invented in 1849 (1) by Levi Strauss (1). He created jeans because gold miners had told him that they wanted pants that didn't rip and wear out easily while they were mining (1).

2. He was a tailor (1) who asked a blacksmith to put copper rivets on a pair of miner's pants (1) so that the pockets would stop ripping (1). So many people liked his idea that Davis talked to Levi Strauss (1); they became partners (1) on a patent for jeans.

3. Strauss decided to make pants using a heavy cloth made in Genoa, Italy (1). People began mispronouncing *Genoa* as *jean* (1); the name stuck (1).

4. They were sturdy (1) and withstood the stresses of gold mining (1). Word of the pants' durability spread (1), and the orders poured in.

5. Jeans are very popular (1). Most Americans own a pair (1); each year, Americans spend billions of dollars on them (1); and more than 400 million pairs are purchased worldwide (1). Today's Levis look similar to the originals (1); they have the trademark of two horses trying to pull apart a pair of jeans (1).

Passage #3: Penicillin

1. The first antibiotic was penicillin (1). Alexander Fleming (1) discovered it as a green mold in a dish of bacteria (2) in September, 1928 (1).

2. Since germs are living cells (1), penicillin breaks through the germ cell wall (1) and causes the cell matter to flow out of the cell (1), killing it (1).

3. Penicillin was tested first on white mice (1) and rabbits (1); and finally, it was tested on a human (1)—Fleming's assistant, Stuart Craddock (1 point for name OR job title).

4. Dr. Chain (1) and Professor Florey (1) convinced the U.S. to produce penicillin to treat soldiers' infected wounds (1) during World War II (1).

5. The child would have died without it (1). It started the use of antibiotics for nonmilitary people (2).

Passage #4: Satellites

1. The Earth (or any planet in our solar system) is a satellite orbiting the sun (1). The moon is a satellite orbiting Earth (1).

2. All artificial satellites have instruments to take measurements (1), cameras (1), solar cells (1), computers (1), control units to perform instructions from Earth (1), and communications units to send information back down to Earth (1).

3. Multistage rockets boost satellites into outer space (1). Each rocket stage fires in turn, then falls away after depleting its fuel (1), until just the satellite remains (1).

4. The satellite's orbit must match the pull of Earth's gravity to hold the satellite in place (1). Each satellite must be placed at an exact height and speed (1). Depending on their purpose, some satellites must stay close to Earth while others must stay very far away (1).

5. Environmental satellites (1) measure pollution in the atmosphere and holes in the ozone layer and watch oceans, icebergs, volcanoes, deserts, forests fires, and moving animal herds such as whales (any 1 = 1 pt.). Military (spy) satellites (1) watch missile sites and the movement of armies and navies (1). Weather satellites (1) record cloud movements and wind speeds (1). Navigational satellites (1) allow vehicles to know their precise location on the Earth's surface whether at sea or on land (1). Astronomical satellites (1) keep track of stars, comets, and meteors (1).

Magazine Articles *(cont.)*

Answer Key *(cont.)*

Passage #5: Lightning

1. Many people are afraid of lightning because it can destroy things like buildings and trees (1), kill people and animals (1), and start dangerous fires (1). Lightning can sometimes strike large airplanes (1). A lightning bolt is hotter than the surface of the sun (1).

2. Lightning helps our planet because every lightning bolt produces ozone gas (1), which protects us from the sun's radiation (1). Lightning also cleans the air (1) by causing pollution particles in the air to fall to the ground (1).

3. Lightning can occur during snowstorms (1), sandstorms (1), tornadoes (1), and volcanic eruptions (1).

4. After every flash of lightning there is a resulting thunderclap (1). The reason is that the sudden heat of a bolt of lightning makes moist air explode outward (1), causing the sound that we call thunder (1).

5. I disagree (1)! Lightning can strike the same place many, many times (1). In fact, the Empire State Building is struck more than 20 times each year (1). Also, lightning strikes areas near the equator very often due to all the warm, moist air that's always there (1).

Passage #6: Diamonds

1. Diamonds form in the Earth's mantle (1) where intense temperatures and high pressure (1) cause carbon to crystallize (1). Over thousands of years the diamonds are pushed closer to the Earth's surface by earthquakes and volcanic eruptions (1).

2. The two largest diamond mines on Earth were found in 1867 (1) in South Africa (1) and in 1979 (1) in Western Australia (1).

3. Diamonds are used in jewelry such as engagement rings, wedding rings, earrings, necklaces, and bracelets (any 1 = 1). Industries use diamonds to cut, grind, and shape hard materials (any 2 = *2 points*).

4. Facets are sides that are cut on a diamond (1). Facets enhance a diamond's ability to reflect and bend light rays (1). Each facet must be cut exactly the right size (1), shape (1), and angle (1) to get the desired effect.

5. Rare diamonds come in yellow, pink, blue, black, brown, green, purple, and red (Any 4 = 4).

Passage #7: Redwood Trees

1. Many people know that redwood trees grow taller than any other living thing on Earth (1). It is also well known that redwood trees can live for thousands of years (1), longer than any other living thing on Earth.

2. Redwood lumber does not rot when exposed to weather (1), instead it turns a pretty shade of red (1). Redwood lumber does not get eaten by termites (1) and is not easily destroyed by fire (1). One redwood tree can provide half a million board feet of lumber (1).

3. During a forest fire, the redwood trees' bark may burn, but the core of the trees will survive (1). Since their bark is so thick and fire resistant (1), they can even withstand temperatures of thousands of degrees! Damage to a redwood tree caused by a forest fire may take more than a hundred years to heal, but it will heal (1).

4. Conservationists are concerned about the redwood trees because most of the remaining trees are owned by lumber companies (1). They fear that the lumber companies will cut them all down (1), so the conservationists have managed to get 70,000 acres of redwood forest turned into public parks (1).

5. I agree that redwood trees are hardy because they are immune to diseases (1), parasites (1), insects (1), and fungi (1). They are even fire resistant and will heal themselves if damaged by a fire (1). If they are cut down or blown down, new saplings will spring up (1). As far as we know, none of them have died of old age (1).

Passage #8: Barn Owls

1. Barn owls received their name because long ago farmers built small openings near their barn roofs to encourage the owls to nest in their barns (1). Farmers welcomed the owls because they ate the rats and mice that destroyed the grain stored in the barns (1).

2. Barn owls have white, heart-shaped faces (1); a keen sense of hearing (1); eyes that can see in the dark (1); strong talons (1); tiny, 1-pound bodies (1); 18-inch-long bodies (1); and wingspans of 40 inches (1). (Any 5 = 5 pts.)

3. Barn owls like to eat voles (1), rats (1), mice (1), frogs (1), little birds (1), and chipmunks (1). (Any 3 = 3 pts.)

4. The barn owls mate (1). The female lays eggs (1) and sits on them for four weeks (1). The male brings her all her food during that time (1). When the eggs hatch, both parents must hunt to provide all the food their growing owlets need (1). After 8 to 10 weeks, the owlets leave the nest (1).

5. Many barn owls die of starvation (1), are hit by cars (1), or get electrocuted by electrical wires (1). Other dangers are goshawks (1) and the increasing use of pesticides (1). (Any 4 = 4 pts.)

Magazine Articles *(cont.)*

Answer Key *(cont.)*

Passage #9: Strawberries

1. In spring, existing strawberry plants grow new leaves (1). Then they put more roots into the earth (1) to get more water and nutrients. Next the plants' leaves spread out to get the maximum possible sunlight (1).

2. Bees pollinate the blossom (1). The blossom's petals fall off (1), and the middle section begins to swell up into a strawberry (1). The tiny strawberry starts out green, then turns white, and finally a ripe red (1). Then it can be picked and eaten (1).

3. Strawberry plants reproduce when their ripe strawberries fall to the ground (1). When the seeds touch the soil, they begin new plants (1). A second way that strawberries reproduce is when the plant sends out a runner with a bud on the end (1). Once the bud opens, a tiny plant puts roots into the ground (1). Even so, the runner continues to get nourishment from the mother plant until autumn (1).

4. The reasons strawberries are so popular in America are they provide vitamin C (1), fiber (1), and protein (1). They have almost no fat (1) and taste terrific (1). (any 4 = 4 points)

5. I disagree. Although California grows most of the strawberries eaten in America (1), most people in the world eat strawberries grown in their own country (1), since strawberries grow all over the world (1).

Passage #10: Komodo Dragons

1. Komodo dragons look very frightening because they have claws the length of adult human fingers (1); thick scales that look like knight's armor (1); and sharp, jagged-edged teeth (1). Another thing that makes them look scary is the fact that they're the largest lizards in the world (1), growing up to 10 feet long (1) and weighing up to 300 pounds (1).

2. Komodo dragons smell prey by continuously flicking their tongue in and out (1). Once they've found prey, they track it silently (1), then charge it (1). They grab the prey with their long claws and jagged teeth (1). Even if the prey escapes, it will die within a few days anyway because of the bacterial infection caused by the bite wound (1).

3. Adult dragons will eat baby dragons (1), so the babies hide in treetops (1) and come down to eat the scraps left over from an adult dragon's kill only after all the adult dragons have gone away (1).

4. Life is difficult for the people who live near the komodo dragons because the dragons will eat them if they're not careful (1). In fact, they must build their homes on stilts to avoid dragon attacks (1). When a loved one dies, the relatives must cover the grave with boulders so that the dragons won't dig up and eat the dead body (1).

5. I disagree. Komodo dragons live on only one island (1), Komodo Island (1), located between Australia and Southeast Asia (1).

Passage #11: Wheat

1. Wheat gives more nourishment to more people than any other food in the world (1). It can grow almost anywhere (1) and is harvested every month of the year somewhere in the world (1). In America, most people eat about 100 pounds of wheat products every single year (1).

2. After the seed is planted in the ground, it sends out tiny roots (1). Then a shoot comes up through the soil and grows leaves (1). Next the shoot sends up spikes (1), each of which grows a head (1). When the kernels in these heads get ripe, the wheat is harvested (1).

3. The wheat is taken from the combine and put into a truck (1), which carries it to a grain elevator for storage (1). Eventually, it is taken from the storage elevator to a mill to be made into flour (1). It travels from the grain elevator to the mill by train, truck, or river barge (1).

4. Once the wheat reaches the mill, it is cleaned by running through sorting discs (1), past a magnet (1), and then washed (1). Next, the grains pass between heavy rollers that break them into tiny pieces (1). These pieces go through sorting screens to separate bran from the kernels (1). Then rollers crush the pieces into flour (1). Finally the flour is run through a sieve just before packaging (1).

Passage #12: Sea Horses

1. Sea horses have many interesting physical characteristics, which include a head shaped like a horse's (1); eyes that move separately (1); a long, flexible tail capable of grasping (1); internal and external skeletons (1); a long snout (1); a tiny dorsal fin on its back (1); and a swim bladder (1). Male sea horses also have a unique pouch for carrying eggs (1). (Any 5 = 5 pts.)

2. A female sea horse lays her eggs into a pouch on the male sea horse's body (1). The male sea horse carries these eggs in his pouch for six weeks (1), then labors to give birth to tiny, live sea horses (1).

3. Sea horses are found in warm, tropical salt water (1). Where a sea horse lives does make a difference in its size (1). Small sea horses live off the Florida coast, in the Gulf of Mexico, and the Caribbean Sea (any 1 = 1). Larger sea horses live off the coasts of California, Australia, and New Zealand (any 1 = 1).

4. A sea horse's enemies are dogfish (1), sharks (1), eels (1), barracudas (1), sting rays (1), and sea turtles (1). (any 4 = 4 points)

5. A person might buy a sea horse for his/her aquarium because sea horses do well in an artificial environment (1) and can be tamed (1). When the person puts food into the aquarium, a sea horse will come over and may wrap its tail around the person's finger (1) or allow itself to be touched on the head (1).

Famous Persons
Outline Student Guide

What's Important about a Famous Person?

1. Name: _____

2. When Born: _____ Where Born: _____

3. Lived Where as an Adult? _____

   _____

4. Famous for: _____

   _____

   _____

5. Accomplishments: _____

   _____

   _____

6. Hardships: _____

   _____

7. Family: _____

   _____

8. What Effect His/Her Life Had on History/the World?

   _____

   _____

   _____

   _____

9. When Died: _____ Where Died: _____

   Of What? _____

10. Other Surprising or Interesting Facts: _____

    _____

    _____

    _____

    _____

Famous Persons (cont.)

Graphic Organizer

Name_____

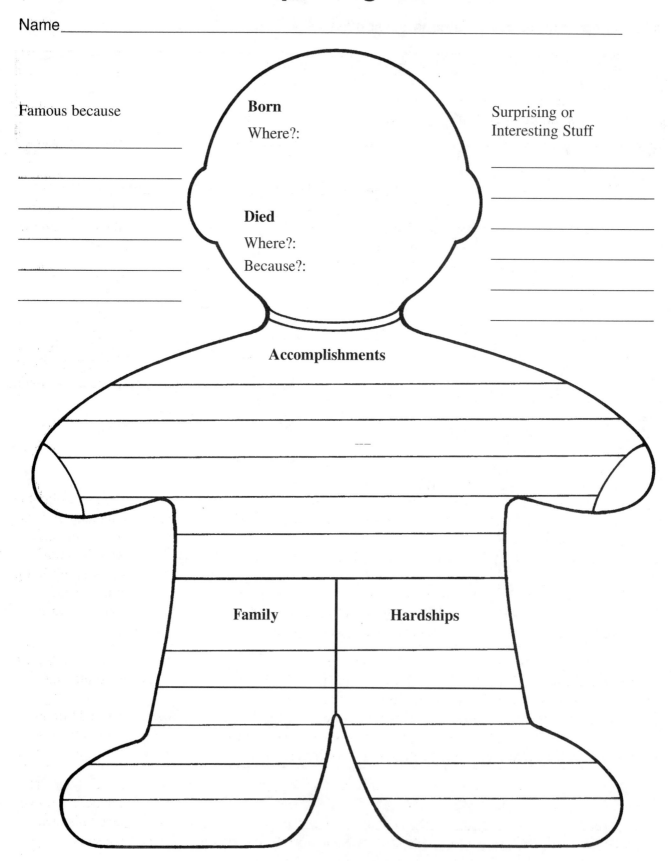

Famous because

_____

_____

_____

_____

_____

Born

Where?:

Died

Where?:

Because?:

Surprising or
Interesting Stuff

_____

_____

_____

_____

_____

Accomplishments

Family

Hardships

Famous Persons (cont.)

Passage #1

Model the use of the outline on page 99 for this passage.

Here are some words you will need to know as you listen about this famous person:

innovative: unique and creative
symphony hall: theater used for musical performances

I. M. Pei, one of the most well-known architects in the world, has given the world innovative structures and earned a reputation for unique geometric designs. When designing anything, his first priority is to ensure that the building will relate to its surroundings in a pleasing way. When designing additions for existing structures, he has demonstrated an exceptional talent at blending the new with the old in unique, yet harmonious ways. Nowhere is this more apparent than the expansion he did on the world-famous Louvre Art Museum in France. Originally a palace, the Louvre had already stood for almost 800 years. At first, the French people were outraged at the idea of an addition, but when they saw Pei's clever designs, many felt the beauty of the ancient building would actually be enhanced by his addition. Their confidence was well-placed, for when the excavation unearthed some original castle walls, rather than rigidly sticking to his carefully made blueprints, he immediately changed his plans to make these walls a permanent display within the museum.

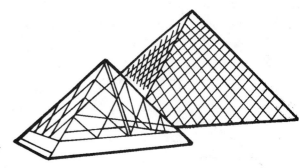

Pei is also known for many other important building projects, including the expansion of Columbia University and a terminal at JFK International Airport, both in New York City. Other famous buildings that boast his handiwork include the National Center for Atmospheric Research in Boulder, Colorado; the John Hancock Tower in Boston; the East Building of the National Gallery of Art in Washington, D.C.; a symphony hall in Dallas; and one of the tallest buildings in the world—the 72-story Hong Kong Bank. One of his most recent accomplishments was the Rock and Roll Hall of Fame in Cleveland, Ohio. In addition to buildings, Pei has designed entire sections of cities, including the business district of Oklahoma City and a neighborhood of low-cost housing for New York City residents.

In April of 1917 Ieoh Ming Pei was born into a wealthy family in Canton, China. His parents sent him to America because they wanted him to have the best education available. He disappointed his father by refusing to become a doctor as the older man wished, instead earning an architectural degree from Harvard University in 1946. Impressed by his ability, the University immediately asked him to teach courses in architecture, which he did for two years. Then he embarked upon a profession as an architectural designer, gaining worldwide admiration throughout his career.

During college, his fraternity brothers called him I. M., and he has used that name ever since. He married Eileen Loo, another Chinese immigrant, in 1942; and together they had two daughters and two sons. In 1954 the entire family became naturalized U.S. citizens. One year later he opened his own architectural firm. Today his firm employs over 200 architects, two of which are his own sons.

Famous Persons (cont.)

Passage #1 Questions

1. When and where was I. M. Pei born? (*3 points*)

   _____

   _____

2. For what kind of designs is I. M. Pei particularly well-known? (*4 points*)

   _____

   _____

   _____

3. What did I. M. Pei change as a result of the Louvre excavation? Why did he make this change? (*2 points*)

   _____

   _____

   _____

4. Name I. M. Pei's architectural accomplishments. (*7 points*)

   _____

   _____

   _____

   _____

5. Explain why you agree or disagree with this statement:

   During his career I. M. Pei has only designed buildings. (*4 points*)

   _____

   _____

   _____

   _____

Famous Persons *(cont.)*

Passage #2

Use the outline on page 99 for this passage.

Here are some words you will need to know as you listen about this famous person:

astronomy: study of the universe, including planets, stars, etc.
candidates: applicants
biology: study of living things

Ten years after Colonel Guy Bluford became the first African-American man to go into space, an African-American woman followed. In September 1992, when the Space Shuttle *Endeavor* lifted off from its launching pad in Cape Canaveral, Florida, one of the seven astronauts aboard this craft was a 35-year-old African-American mission specialist, Dr. Mae Jemison. As a medical doctor, she did experiments on the effects of gravity on the human body in a pressurized laboratory while orbiting the earth at nearly 18,000 miles per hour. In addition, Jemison studied bone cells and developmental biology by hatching 150 frog eggs in the weightless atmosphere of outer space. Her other experiments focused on ways to reduce space sickness, a form of motion sickness similar to seasickness.

Jemison was born in October of 1956. Throughout her childhood in Chicago, she followed the Apollo and Gemini space missions with great interest and hoped that someday she, too, would travel in space. Her parents believed strongly in the importance of education and encouraged all three of their children to spend hours in the library reading. Jemison chose to read about astronomy and science fiction. When she finished high school at 16, she won a scholarship to study at Stanford University. There she received a degree in chemical engineering. Then she furthered her studies by earning a medical degree from Cornell University Medical College. Jemison worked for the next few years as a doctor for the Peace Corps, providing medical care to people in the African countries of Liberia and Sierra Leone.

In 1985 she opened her own medical practice in California, took some graduate courses in biomedical engineering, and applied to be an astronaut. Out of 2,000 candidates, Jemison was one of the 15 selected for NASA's training program. Since the mission on which she served was a joint project between America and Japan, part of her training occurred in Japan, where she added Japanese to the three languages she already spoke fluently.

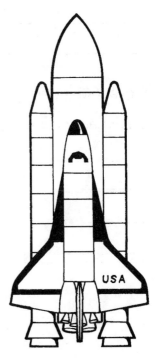

To symbolize her belief that space belongs to all nations, she carried several small art objects from West African countries into space. Upon her return from her seven-day flight aboard Endeavor, Jemison received a homecoming party hosted by 8,000 schoolchildren. A mural at the Lambert-St. Louis International Airport entitled "Black Americans in Flight" honors her as the first African-American woman in space. Today she works as a Dartmouth College professor, teaching courses on space technology and third-world nations.

Famous Persons *(cont.)*

Passage #2 Questions

1. During her childhood, how did Mae Jemison begin preparing herself to become an astronaut? *(3 points)*

_____

_____

_____

2. Tell about the things Mae Jemison did aboard the space shuttle Endeavor. *(4 points)*

_____

_____

_____

_____

3. Give examples of how Mae Jemison used intelligence and hard work to achieve so much before the age of 40. *(7 points)*

_____

_____

_____

_____

_____

_____

4. What were Mae Jemison's three different careers? *(3 points)*

_____

_____

_____

5. Why might Mae Jemison be a role model to others? *(3 points)*

_____

_____

_____

Famous Persons *(cont.)*

Passage #3

Model the use of the graphic organizer on page 100 for this passage.

> Here are some words you will need to know as you listen about this famous person:
>
> **Baroque music:** religious music with many complex details and contrasts
> **composer:** a person who creates new music
> **ancestors:** relatives from long ago (for example, your great-grandfather)

The famous musical composer named Johann Sebastian Bach was born in 1685 in Eisenach, Germany. Bach is considered the genius of Baroque music. He was the most successful composer of his era, managing to support a very large family with his musical talent.

From an early age, Bach, who had many musically talented ancestors, showed a talent for music. At four, his father began teaching him to play the violin. When he was orphaned at the age of 10 he went to live with his eldest brother, Christopher. In addition to teaching him how to read music, Christopher taught Bach how to play the harpsichord and clavichord.

Through the recommendation of his school headmaster, Bach won a scholarship to study music at St. Michael's when he was just 15 years old. Eager to learn but lacking transportation, he walked over 200 miles to reach the school. There he learned to play the pipe organ for church services, becoming so accomplished that he could play complex music from memory.

Johann Sebastian Bach

In 1707 Bach returned home and married his cousin, Maria Barbara Bach. They had seven children, four of whom grew up to become famous musical composers themselves. In 1720 Bach's wife died, and the following year he married Anna Magdalena Wilcken. They had 13 children, only six of whom survived infancy. His second wife was a singer who spent many hours carefully copying Bach's compositions. It is due to her efforts that much of his music has survived over the centuries.

In 1749 Bach, whose eyesight had been failing for some time, went completely blind. A doctor performed two surgeries, but both attempts failed and Bach's overall health deteriorated rapidly. For a single day in July of 1750 he regained his sight, but tragically he suffered a stroke within hours and died ten days later.

Bach's complete works, nearly 300 of which were choral cantatas, would fill 60 volumes if some had not been lost or destroyed through the more than two centuries since his death.

Famous Persons (cont.)

Passage #3 Questions

1. How do you know that Johann Sebastian Bach was determined to learn all he could about music? (*4 points*)

_____

_____

_____

2. Name the hardships that Johann Sebastian Bach faced during his life. (*5 points*)

_____

_____

_____

3. What did Bach's second wife do that was significant? (*4 points*)

_____

_____

_____

4. How old was Bach when he died? What was his cause of death? (*3 points*)

_____

_____

_____

5. What is Johann Sebastian Bach remembered for? (*4 points*)

_____

_____

_____

Famous Persons *(cont.)*

Passage #4

Use the graphic organizer on page 100 for this passage.

Here are some words you will need to know as you listen about this famous person:

impoverished: extremely poor
prejudice: an unreasonable, negative opinion of another
gender: being male or female

Most people remember the Cherokee because of the tragic Trail of Tears—that time in 1838 when 13,000 Cherokee had to leave their land in the southeast woodlands of Oklahoma to go to Indian Territory almost 1,000 miles away. The people were allowed to take nothing with them, and they had to travel on foot. An estimated 4,000 died during the extremely difficult journey, but about 1,000 tribe members managed to hide in the Great Smoky Mountains, which form a natural boundary between Tennessee and North Carolina. Since that time, members of the Cherokee Nation have sought to rebuild the territory they lost. Wilma Mankiller made great strides in doing just that.

Wilma Mankiller was born into an impoverished family of 11 children in Oklahoma in 1945. When she met a group of Native-American activists in college, she realized that she wanted to serve the people of her tribe, the Cherokee. In 1983 the chief candidate, Ross Swimmer, asked her to run as his deputy chief. She accepted his offer but then had to overcome extreme prejudice because of her gender. She received threatening letters and phone calls and had her tires slashed. Still, Swimmer was elected with Mankiller at his side. In 1985 when Swimmer left his post to accept a position in Washington, D.C., Mankiller became the first woman to serve as the chief of the ancient Cherokee Nation, the second largest Native-American tribe in the United States today. While chief, Mankiller built health clinics, reworked the justice system, and helped construct a 16-mile-long water pipeline to bring indoor plumbing for the first time to some of her tribal members. Her actions brought her Nation greater political weight in the United States than ever before and helped her to realize a lifelong dream to teach others about the Cherokee culture. She won strong victories in both 1987 and 1991 and continued to lead throughout two life-threatening illnesses and a kidney transplant.

She worked hard to preserve the history, traditions, and customs of the Cherokee Nation, as well as to obtain for her people a more important place in American society. Under her leadership, the people regained many of their traditions and much of the pride that had vanished over the years. For her efforts, Wilma Mankiller was inducted into the Oklahoma Women's Hall of Fame in 1986, received an honorary doctorate from the University of New England, and was named as one of the United States' outstanding women leaders in 1993.

Famous Persons (cont.)

Passage #4 Questions

1. Tell what you know about the Cherokee Nation's history. (*5 points*)

_____

_____

_____

_____

_____

2. When and where was Wilma Mankiller born? (*2 points*)

_____

_____

3. Describe specific ways the Cherokee tribe has benefited by having Wilma Mankiller as their chief. (*6 points*)

_____

_____

_____

_____

_____

4. Over the years Wilma Mankiller has faced several problems that would have made it easier for her to quit working for her tribe than to continue. What were these problems? (*5 points*)

_____

_____

_____

_____

5. What honors has Mankiller received? (*2 points*)

_____

_____

Famous Persons (cont.)

Passage #5

Do not use the student guide pages for this passage.

> Here are some words you will need to know as you listen about this famous person:
>
> **recurring:** occurring again and again
> **inducted:** added to

Roberto Clemente, one of the most popular baseball players of all time, was born in Carolina, Puerto Rico, in 1934 to a poor family. Clemente's family gave him solid values, teaching him to share with others, always tell the truth, and work hard. Although his family could not afford to buy a real baseball, he and his friends made their own by wrapping string around old golf balls they'd found.

Clemente loved baseball and played at every opportunity. He couldn't wait to enter high school because they had real baseball equipment. Clemente made his school's baseball all-star team three years in a row. After high school, he joined the Santurce Crabbers baseball team in Puerto Rico, then later went to Montreal, Canada, to play on a farm team. There, scouts from the major leagues saw him play, and in 1954 he signed a contract to play right field for the Pittsburgh Pirates.

A quiet, sensitive man, he always gave 100 percent to his team, even when he had recurring pain from muscle problems. In both 1960 and 1971, Roberto helped the Pirates win World Series championships. In 1961 he had the highest batting average in the National League—a feat which he repeated three more times in his career—and in 1966 he was voted Most Valuable Player of the National League. On September 30, 1972, he became one of only a dozen players in the history of baseball to achieve 3,000 hits. His lifetime batting average was .317, and he is widely considered the greatest defensive right fielder of all time.

Although baseball took a great deal of his time, Clemente always found time to help those in need. He visited sick children and donated money to help others. When an earthquake struck Nicaragua in December 1972, he spent his Christmas vacation organizing a relief committee to aid the victims. He set out to deliver the supplies personally, but the Nicaraguans never received them. Just minutes after takeoff from San Juan Airport, his heavily loaded airplane crashed into the ocean. The people of Puerto Rico grieved at the loss of their fallen hero.

Shortly after his death, he was inducted into the National Baseball Hall of Fame. His young widow and three small sons decided to fulfill a lifelong dream of Clemente's, so in the early 1980s they opened a sports complex in his name for the children of Puerto Rico.

Famous Persons (cont.)

Passage #5 Questions

1. When and where was Roberto Clemente born? (*2 points*)

_____

_____

2. Give some examples of how you know that Roberto was born into poverty. (*2 points*)

_____

_____

_____

3. List the accomplishments Roberto Clemente achieved during his lifetime. (*5 points*)

_____

_____

_____

_____

_____

4. How do you know that Roberto was concerned with the needs of others? (*7 points*)

_____

_____

_____

_____

5. What two important events occurred after Roberto Clemente's tragic death? (*4 points*)

_____

_____

_____

Famous Persons (cont.)

Passage #6

Do not use the student guide pages for this passage.

Here are some words you will need to know as you listen about this famous person:

plantation: a farm so large that it requires many workers to operate it
alternately: switching back and forth between two things

Born a slave on a plantation in Maryland around 1820, Harriett Tubman was the sixth of 11 children living in a one-room hut with a dirt floor and no windows. By the time she turned five, she worked in the fields; and by the age of eight, she cared for a newborn infant 24 hours a day on a neighboring plantation.

Early in her teen years, Harriet stepped between a master chasing a runaway slave. The furious man threw a flat iron at her, striking her in the head and almost killing her. She suffered from severe headaches and unconscious spells for the rest of her life. The injury served as a turning point for her. She became deeply religious and decided that even if it cost her her life, she would someday be free.

In 1844 Harriett married a free man, John Tubman. She told him of her dream for freedom, but he told her to forget about it. Then when she told him of her plans to run away, he threatened to tell her master. One night in 1849, she did escape with three of her brothers, but their intense fear forced them to turn back. Two nights later, she escaped alone to the home of a white woman who had offered her assistance. There she discovered the Underground Railroad, a secret network of houses that harbored escaping slaves on their route north to freedom. To avoid capture, Harriett hid at these homes or in barns during the day and traveled only by night until she reached the non-slavery state of Pennsylvania.

Between 1850 and 1860 she earned money by washing dishes, cooking, and cleaning. She used almost every penny she made to make 19 trips south to lead over 300 slaves to freedom on the Underground Railroad. Posters offering huge sums of money for her capture—dead or alive—appeared all over the South, but no one caught her since she alternately disguised herself as a man or an old woman.

Once runaway slaves started north with her, Harriett would not allow them to turn back. She would point a gun at their heads and say, "You'll go on or die." She never had to pull the trigger, and she never lost a single "passenger" to slave hunters. People began calling her Moses because she led so many of her people out of slavery.

During the Civil War, Harriett served as a nurse and a spy for soldiers in the Union Army. When all the slaves were freed at the end of the war, she settled in Auburn, New York, where she established a home for sick, poor, and homeless blacks. She also worked tirelessly to help women earn the right to vote. She was over 90 years old when she died peacefully on March 10, 1913.

Famous Persons (cont.)

Passage #6 Questions

1. What did Harriett Tubman do to avoid being caught by slave catchers? (*5 points*)

_____

_____

_____

2. Did Harriett Tubman's family members help her to escape? What did they do? (*3 points*)

_____

_____

3. When runaway slaves were afraid, would Harriett Tubman allow them to turn back? What would she do and why? (*4 points*)

_____

_____

_____

_____

4. Why did people begin calling Harriett Tubman "Moses"? (*3 points*)

_____

_____

_____

5. Besides her role as "Moses," what else did Harriett Tubman do to help others? (*5 points*)

_____

_____

_____

_____

Famous Persons *(cont.)*

Passage #7

Do not use the student guide pages for this passage.

Here are some words you will need to know as you listen about this famous person:

botany: the study of plants
agriculture: the science of growing crops and raising livestock

---

No one knows George Washington Carver's birthdate because he was orphaned as an infant. His father died in a farming accident immediately after his birth, and his mother was kidnapped by slave raiders and never seen again. Fortunately, Moses and Susan Carver, the couple in Diamond Grove, Missouri, who owned his mother, chased after the raiders and managed to recover George. They then raised George and his older brother James as members of their family.

Even as a toddler, George showed a love of learning and a fascination with nature. At the age of 12, he left the Carvers to find a school that would accept blacks. His travels took him to Missouri, Iowa, and Kansas. Along the way he earned money by doing laundry, farm work, and cooking.

In 1894 George graduated with honors from Iowa State College with a Bachelor's degree in botany. Immediately the administration offered him a post as director of the greenhouse. During this time, he discovered a fungus that grows on the leaves of red and silver maples. From that point on, George's reputation began to grow due to his extensive knowledge of botany and agriculture.

Upon receiving his Master's degree in 1896, he became a professor and the chairperson of the Department of Agriculture at an outstanding college for blacks, the Tuskegee Institute. His work there included plant research and assisting black farmers in growing more abundant crops. For years they had planted cotton; now the soil lacked nutrients, and a type of beetle called boll weevils had infested and destroyed acres of cotton. George purchased a wagon and took his equipment, seeds, and knowledge right to the farmers in their fields. He suggested they plant peanuts. The first season produced such an overabundance of peanuts that no one knew what to do with them. George worked in his lab analyzing peanuts. He developed over 300 peanut-based products, including many used today, such as cooking oil, soap, lotion, soil conditioner, and insulation. After conducting more research over the next 47 years, he found 118 uses for sweet potatoes and over 100 uses for cowpeas.

The National Association for the Advancement of Colored People gave him a medal for his achievement in agricultural chemistry, and two universities awarded him honorary doctor of science degrees. George died on January 5, 1943, and was buried on the campus of Tuskegee Institute. He left money to give scholarships to black students who want to study chemistry, botany, or agriculture in college. In 1948 the U.S. Post Office issued a postage stamp to honor this great American.

Famous Persons (cont.)

Passage #7 Questions

1. What were two hardships that George Washington Carver had to overcome as a child? (*2 points*)

_____

_____

_____

2. How do you know that George Washington Carver was eager for an education? (*4 points*)

_____

_____

_____

3. For what three plants did George Washington Carver find hundreds of uses? (*2 points*)

_____

_____

_____

4. Name seven of the degrees and honors George Washington Carver earned. (*7 points*)

_____

_____

_____

_____

5. Describe the things George Washington Carver did to improve life for other black people. (*5 points*)

_____

_____

_____

_____

_____

Famous Persons (cont.)

Passage #8

Do not use the student guide pages for this passage.

> Here are some words you will need to know as you listen about this famous person:
>
> **laryngitis:** an illness leaving you temporarily unable to speak
> **insignificant:** unimportant
> **recuperate:** recover; get better

Clara Barton discovered her calling in life at the age of 11 when her brother almost died and she nursed him back to health. The youngest of the Barton children, Clara was born on Christmas Day of 1821 in Oxford, Massachusetts. At 17 she began a teaching career, and in 1850 she entered college. Upon completing her studies, she started the first public school in New Jersey by offering to teach without pay. When she got a severe case of laryngitis, she went to Washington, D.C., to recover. There she worked as a government clerk until the Civil War began in 1861.

When the Civil War started, not one trained nurse existed in all of America! Realizing this, Barton requested permission from the War Department to work on the battlefields, but officials considered it an unfit place for a woman. Finally, at her father's funeral, she received word she could travel with the Army of the Potomac.

While caring for injured soldiers, she would work for three days straight with only one meal and an hour and a half of sleep. No matter how exhausted, hungry, or ill she became, she refused to rest if even one wounded man needed care. She burned her hand and got frostbitten fingers but would not stop to tend to her own injuries, thinking them insignificant compared to the soldiers'. Twice, she was nearly shot: one bullet passed though her sleeve and another tore off part of her skirt.

After the war ended, Barton began giving lectures. In 1870 her voice failed her again, and she went to Europe to rest. Instead, she started nursing soldiers on the battlefields of the Franco-Prussian War. She was impressed that the wounded received immediate medical care and food from the International Red Cross. She learned that through the Geneva Treaty, hospitals flying the Red Cross flag could not be attacked and Red Cross personnel would help anyone in need.

Impressed by her efforts during the war, the German emperor awarded Barton the Iron Cross of Merit for Ladies—the first of 27 honors she received during her lifetime. Then she became so ill she almost went blind, so she bought a home in Dansville, New York, and went there to recuperate. As soon as she felt able, she urged the American government to join the International Red Cross. The U.S. government wasn't interested, even though she explained that an American Red Cross could provide assistance for peacetime disasters. The Dansville citizens liked Barton's idea, so they formed the first American Red Cross chapter in August of 1881. Shortly thereafter, forest fires in Michigan left over 5,000 people homeless. Dansville immediately responded, motivating two neighboring cities to start Red Cross chapters.

After seeing the Red Cross in action, President Arthur signed the Geneva Treaty recognizing the International Red Cross on March 1, 1882. That July, he appointed Barton president of the American Red Cross. She stepped down from its leadership at the age of 82 but remained active in the organization until she died from pneumonia at the age of 91.

Famous Persons (cont.)

Passage #8 Questions

1. What events caused Clara Barton to become involved in nursing? (*3 points*)

_____

_____

_____

_____

2. List the jobs Clara Barton held during her life. (*5 points*)

_____

_____

_____

_____

3. Explain how a recurring medical condition caused Clara Barton to change her career twice. (*2 points*)

_____

_____

_____

_____

4. What caused the United States government to finally become interested in the Red Cross? (*3 points*)

_____

_____

_____

5. Tell what you know about the organization for which Clara Barton is remembered. (*7 points*)

_____

_____

_____

_____

Famous Persons *(cont.)*

Passage #9

Do not use the student guide pages for this passage.

> Here are some words you will need to know as you listen about this famous person:
>
> **dowry:** a wedding gift of money or property from a bride to her husband
> **vegetarian:** person who refuses to eat animals
> **rudimentary:** basic

Remembered for having one of the greatest imaginations in history, Leonardo da Vinci was born in Italy on April 15, 1452. His father refused to marry his mother because she could not raise a dowry. Instead, he married a wealthy woman. Although Leonardo's stepmother raised him, he kept in close contact with his birth mother throughout his life.

From an early age, Leonardo had a terrific desire for knowledge. He wanted to discover everything about the world and how it works, so he studied nature. After extensively studying the animal kingdom, Leonardo developed such respect for animal life that he became a vegetarian. At the age of 10, Leonardo studied under Verrocchio, creator of the world-famous statue depicting David with the head of Goliath at his feet. Shortly after Leonardo turned 20, he became Verrocchio's assistant and gave art lessons to Michaelangelo, who later become famous for painting the Sistene Chapel's ceiling. Leonardo left notebooks showing the designs of numerous sculptures he created. Unfortunately, none of these sculptures still exist.

Between the ages of 30 and 47, Leonardo served as chief engineer to the ruler of Milan, creating maps of the region as well as designing a system of canals, bridges, and a steam-fired cannon. During this time, he also painted the two most widely recognized art pieces in the world: *The Last Supper* and the *Mona Lisa*. Then he planned a castle for King Francis I of France and supervised its construction. He also designed a network of canals that never got dug. When Napoleon uncovered his plans more than 300 years later, these canals finally became a reality.

During every spare moment, Leonardo filled more than 10,000 notebook pages with detailed calculations and designs for hundreds of futuristic inventions. He tried creating an airplane 400 years before one came into being. Nearly five centuries before the first helicopter, he drew one. Amazingly, most of these inventions would have worked had he possessed the technical information available today. Leonardo invented an alarm clock, a power loom, a rudimentary air conditioning system, a self-propelled wagon, a paddlewheel boat, gas masks, and a submarine. A fiercely private man, he wrote all descriptions from right to left so that they could only be read by holding them up to a mirror. Leonardo enjoyed working alone, and even after becoming one of the most famous men in Italy he shunned public attention.

Leonardo never married, but in 1490 he adopted a troubled 10-year-old boy who repeatedly stole things from Leonardo and others. Still Leonardo loyally loved him and left him half of the property he owned in Milan when he died. After Leonardo's mother died in 1496, he adopted another son to whom he left his beloved notebooks when he died peacefully on May 2, 1519.

Famous Persons (cont.)

Passage #9 Questions

1. Explain the circumstances surrounding Leonardo da Vinci's birth. (*3 points*)

   _____

   _____

   _____

2. How do you know that Leonardo da Vinci was eager to learn everything he could about the world and how it works? (*4 points*)

   _____

   _____

   _____

   _____

3. Give three examples of how Leonardo da Vinci showed compassion to others. (*3 points*)

   _____

   _____

   _____

   _____

4. What did Leonardo da Vinci do with his notebooks that was strange? Why did he do it? (*5 points*)

   _____

   _____

   _____

   _____

5. What is Leonardo da Vinci remembered for? (*5 points*)

   _____

   _____

   _____

   _____

   _____

Famous Persons *(cont.)*

Passage #10

Do not use the student guide pages for this passage.

> Here are some words you will need to know as you listen about this famous person:
>
> **missionary:** a person who goes to a foreign country for religious reasons
> **slum:** an overcrowded part of a city where the people are very poor
> **humanitarian:** a person who devotes his or her life to helping others

In August 1910 Mother Teresa was born Agnes Bojaxhui in Skopje (Sko-pee-ay) in present-day Yugoslavia. The youngest of three children, she had a happy childhood in spite of her father's death several years after her birth. At 12 she began dreaming of becoming a Roman Catholic nun and joined the Order of Loreto at 18. As part of her new life, she took the name of Saint Teresa and went by that name for the rest of her life.

She went as a missionary to India, assigned to teach in a convent school for rich children in the capital city, Calcutta. When she became principal, she received the title of Mother Teresa. The horrible slum conditions just outside her bedroom window bothered her a great deal. On September 10, 1946, she felt she received a message from God telling her to leave the convent, live among the "poorest of the poor," and help them however she could. Mother Teresa immediately requested permission to follow this call but did not receive her release until 1948. She left the convent with no place to stay and only a few coins. She lived on the streets with the homeless until offered the attic of a person's home.

In December of 1948 she started a school out on a street. One year later, her first helpers—three former students—joined her; and by 1950 she had enough sisters to create a new religious order called the Missionary Sisters of Charity. In 1952 Mother Teresa convinced city officials to give her some unused rooms to create a home for the dying where she and her sisters carried seriously ill people in from the streets, washed them, gave them medical treatment, and administered the last rites of whatever religion they believed in. Three years later she established a home for orphans and abandoned children. In 1957 she opened a place for lepers—people with a dreaded disease that can result in lost limbs. Although she never earned so much as a penny, she always managed to have whatever money she required miraculously appear within 24 hours of needing it.

By 1963 so many men wanted to assist in her work that the Missionary Brothers of Charity was formed; and two years later, additional orders of the Missionaries of Charity began working with the poor and sick in countries throughout the world, including Venezuela, Tanzania, Australia, and even America. By the end of the century, more than 150 such missions helped those in need.

In 1979 she received one of the greatest honors in the world, the Nobel Peace Prize. She donated the $990,000 that came with the award to the poor. The United States honored her with the Presidential Medal of Freedom in 1985. At the time of her death in September 1997, Mother Teresa, perhaps the greatest humanitarian of the twentieth century, owned just two garments, a bucket for washing, a sleeping mat, a Bible, and less than one dollar. She had given not only her life but all her worldly goods to the "poorest of the poor."

Famous Persons (cont.)

Passage #10 Questions

1. What did Mother Teresa do as a result of her message from God? (*4 points*)

   _____

   _____

   _____

2. Where did Mother Teresa spend most of her life working? (*3 points*)

   _____

   _____

   _____

3. In what ways did Mother Teresa demonstrate respect for the people who were dying in the streets? (*4 points*)

   _____

   _____

   _____

   _____

4. Explain how she got the name Mother Teresa. (*3 points*)

   _____

   _____

   _____

5. At the time of her death, what organizations and institutions had Mother Teresa created? (*6 points*)

   _____

   _____

   _____

   _____

Famous Persons (cont.)

Passage #11

Do not use the student guide pages for this passage.

> Here are some words you will need to know as you listen about this famous person:
>
> **blockade:** to totally cut off one area from another by means of force
> **Barbary pirates:** robbers who waited along an important sea route to attack and steal from ships

At the age of 15, John Barry snuck aboard a ship bound for the American colonies and religious freedom. Born in Wexford, Ireland, in 1745, he had grown to hate his British rulers' prejudice against Roman Catholics and hoped to have better opportunities in the new land. Little did he know when he arrived in the city of Philadelphia, Pennsylvania, that he would someday become one of its great historical figures.

Filled with a love for the sea and the American colonies, Barry grew to be a huge man. Throughout his life as a sea captain, he earned a reputation for his daring and bravery, as well as for treating his crew firmly but kindly. A deeply religious man, he had strict rules for his crewmen, including no liquor on the ship and church attendance on Sunday if in port or listening to the Bible read aloud if not in port.

Barry played a significant role in helping America win her freedom from the British during the Revolutionary War and later established the Naval Department of the United States. When the Revolutionary War began, he discovered the British plan to blockade the Delaware River and seize every ship bound to or from the colonies' capitol city of Philadelphia so as to starve the American colonists into submission. He immediately helped change merchant ships into the first Yankee warships ever put to sea. Then he fought the British from a tiny schooner and managed to keep them from controlling the Delaware River. Whenever he was without a ship to command, he set up his guns on shore and joined in the battles of Trenton and Princeton. As commander of the *Lexington*, Barry captured the *Edward*, the first British ship to be taken in combat by the newborn Continental Navy; and he later fired the last shot at sea of the Revolutionary War, in 1783.

When the Revolutionary War ended, he worked tirelessly to convince the United States government of the need for a standing navy to defend her shores. Through the Constitution, he was appointed captain of the first American navy in 1794. He personally trained many of the men who served in the navy during the War of 1812 as well as those who finally defeated the Barbary pirates.

By 1906 Philadelphia had erected two statues in honor of Barry, and President Theodore Roosevelt had another statue placed in his honor in Washington, D.C. In 1956 the American government paid further tribute to his achievements by giving Ireland a bronze statue of him, which today stands in his birthplace. Although he left no children when he died in 1803 at age 58, he will forever be remembered as the "Father of the American Navy" for his courage and determination to establish a standing naval force for the United States of America.

Famous Persons (cont.)

Passage #11 Questions

1. Why did John Barry leave the land where he had been born? (*4 points*)

   _____

   _____

   _____

2. Tell about John Barry's treatment of the sailors who served under his command. What were his rules? (*4 points*)

   _____

   _____

   _____

   _____

3. What significant role did John Barry play in the Revolutionary War? (*4 points*)

   _____

   _____

   _____

   _____

4. How many statues are there of John Barry and where are they located? (*4 points*)

   _____

   _____

   _____

5. Name the reasons why John Barry is considered the "Father of the American Navy." (*4 points*)

   _____

   _____

   _____

   _____

Famous Persons *(cont.)*

Passage #12

Do not use the student guide pages for this passage.

Here are some words you will need to know as you listen about this famous person:

attorney general: the chief lawyer for a major government
majority leader: the head of the main political party in government
legislature: elected officials who make our laws
interpretation: what one understands something to mean

While growing up in the 1930s on an isolated cattle ranch in Arizona, Sandra Day O'Connor had no idea she would one day sit on the most important court in the land. During the school year, she lived with her grandparents in El Paso, Texas in order to go to school. An excellent student, O'Connor graduated high school at 16 and enrolled in Stanford University to study economics because she hoped someday to operate her parents' ranch. Then she decided to try law school. In 1952 she graduated third in her class at the age of 22. However, when she looked for a job as a lawyer, no one wanted to hire her because she was a woman.

While studying to become a lawyer, O'Connor had met her husband. They married in 1952 and had three sons. She stayed home with her children for five years. Then in 1965 she received the position of assistant attorney general for the state of Arizona. Four years later she began serving as a senator in the Arizona state legislature. In 1972 she made history when the Arizona Republican senators asked her to serve as the first female majority leader in a state legislature.

In 1974 she left the political arena to become a trial judge for a county court, where she listened to cases for five years. Then she moved into a position as judge for the Arizona Court of Appeals, where she alone decided cases without a jury. Since women couldn't even vote until 1920, O'Connor's achievements are truly amazing.

Sandra Day O'Connor made history yet again when she became the first female justice appointed to the United States Supreme Court in September of 1981. As the highest court in the nation, the Supreme Court receives requests to hear almost 5,000 cases annually. At least four of the nine judges must want to hear a case for it to be presented at the next term. During each term, which runs from October to June, the Court listens to about 150 cases. Sometimes O'Connor is one of at least five judges who agrees to make the ruling on a case. Then O'Connor may write the majority opinion. When she disagrees with the majority, she may write her own opinion statement explaining why she believes in a different interpretation of the law. Since a Supreme Court justice receives a lifetime appointment, O'Connor may choose to serve in this very important position until she dies.

Famous Persons (cont.)

Passage #12 Questions

1. Did Sandra Day O'Connor live with her parents year round when she was a child? If not, who did she live with, and why? (*3 points*)

_____

_____

_____

2. How did Sandra Day O'Connor's dreams change when she went to college? (*3 points*)

_____

_____

_____

3. How does Sandra Day O'Connor's career show the changes that have occurred for American women during her lifetime? (*4 points*)

_____

_____

_____

_____

4. Sandra Day O'Connor made American history as the first female in which two important political positions? (*2 points*)

_____

_____

5. Describe Sandra Day O'Connor's role on the United States Supreme Court. (*8 points*)

_____

_____

_____

_____

Famous Persons *(cont.)*

Use this scoring guide in conjunction with the answer key to assess student performance.

Scoring Guide			
Points Possible	**Exemplary Score**	**Average Score**	**Minimum Passing Score**
20	17–20	14–16	12

Answer Key

Passage #1: I. M. Pei

1. I. M. Pei was born in 1917 (1) in Canton (1), China (1).

2. I. M. Pei is well-known for his unique designs (1) and use of geometric shapes (1). He has a particular talent for making buildings fit in with their surroundings (1) and additions blend with the original structure (1).

3. I. M. Pei changed his plans for the Louvre Art Museum when old castle walls were discovered (1). He did this so that the walls could become a permanent display for the museum (1).

4. I. M. Pei's many accomplishments include the addition to the Louvre (1); the expansion of Columbia University (1); a terminal at JFK International Airport (1); the National Center for Atmospheric Research (1); the John Hancock Tower (1); the East Building of the National Gallery of Art (1); a symphony hall (1); the Rock and Roll Hall of Fame (1); and one of the tallest building in the world, the Hong Kong Bank (1). He also designed entire sections of cities (1). He started an architectural firm (1). (Any 7 = 7 pts.)

5. I disagree with this statement (1) because I. M. Pei designed whole sections of cities (1). He did these designs for Oklahoma City (1) and New York City (1).

Passage #2: Mae Jemison

1. As a child, Mae Jemison read a lot about astronomy and science fiction (1). She followed the Apollo and Gemini space missions closely (2).

2. Mae Jemison did experiments on the effects of gravity on the human body (1), and she studied bone cells (1) and developmental biology (1). She tried to find ways to reduce space sickness (1).

3. As a child she read a great deal about astronomy (1). She graduated from high school early (1), and her good grades earned her a scholarship (1). She got a degree in chemical engineering (1), then went on to become a doctor (1). Later she took courses in biomedical engineering (1). She became fluent in four languages (1).

4. Mae Jemison worked as a medical doctor (1), astronaut (1), and is currently a college professor (1).

5. Mae Jemison achieved a lot at a young age. She fulfilled her dreams through education and hard work (1). This can motivate other people to work hard and get a good education to fulfill their dreams, too (2).

Passage #3: Johann Sebastian Bach

1. Bach learned how to read music (1), as well as how to play four musical instruments (1). Bach was willing to walk 200 miles to get to a musical scholarship (2).

2. Bach was orphaned at ten (1). His first wife died (1). At least seven of his children died in infancy (1). He went blind (1). He won a scholarship but had to walk 200 miles to get there (1).

3. Bach's second wife had 13 children (1). She was a singer (1). She copied his musical compositions, which is why so many have survived the centuries (2).

4. Bach was 65 years old (2), and he died after having a stroke (1).

5. Bach is the genius of Baroque music (1). He composed 60 volumes of music (1). He composed 300 choral cantatas (1). He was the most successful composer of his era (1).

Passage #4: Wilma Mankiller

1. In 1838 the Cherokee had to leave their land (1) and travel by foot to Indian territory almost a thousand miles away (1). They could take nothing with them (1), and the journey was so difficult that thousands died making it (1). The path they took is called the Trail of Tears (1).

2. She was born into the Cherokee tribe in Oklahoma (1) in 1945 (1).

3. The Cherokee tribe has benefited by having Mankiller as their chief because she built health clinics (2), reworked the justice system (2), and helped construct a water pipeline to bring indoor plumbing to some of her tribal members (2) for the first time.

4. Wilma Mankiller had to overcome prejudice because she was a female leader (1). She received threats (1) and had her tires slashed (1). She had two very serious illnesses (1) and a kidney transplant (1).

5. Mankiller was added to the Oklahoma Women's Hall of Fame in 1986 (1) and was named as one of the United States' outstanding women leaders in 1993 (1). She also received an honorary doctorate from University of New England (1). (Any 2 = 2 pts.)

Famous Persons *(cont.)*

Answer Key *(cont.)*

Passage #5: Roberto Clemente

1. Roberto Clemente was born in 1934 (1) in Carolina, Puerto Rico (1).

2. He had to make his own baseballs because his family couldn't afford to buy him one (1). He couldn't wait to go to high school because they had real baseball equipment (1).

3. Roberto Clemente had the highest batting average in his league four times (1), and he was the Most Valuable Player in 1966 (1). He made 3,000 hits (1), and his lifetime batting average was .317 (1). He helped the Pittsburgh Pirates achieve World Series victories in 1960 and 1971 (1).

4. He visited sick children (2) and donated money to help others (2). He died trying to deliver supplies that he had collected to help earthquake victims (2). Roberto's lifelong dream was to open a sports complex for Puerto-Rican children (1).

5. Roberto was inducted into the Baseball Hall of Fame (2), and his family opened a sports complex for the children of Puerto Rico (2).

Passage #6: Harriet Tubman

1. She used the Underground Railroad (1), travelling by night (1) and hiding during the day (1). She sometimes wore the disguise of a man (1) and sometimes of an old woman (1).

2. No, they did not (1). They actually prevented her from running away! Her brothers forced her to turn back from her first attempt to flee (1), and her husband threatened to tell her master if she tried to run away (1).

3. No (1). Harriett would put a gun to their heads and threaten to kill them (1). Fortunately, she never had to shoot anyone. She did this because she knew that if they returned they might reveal the Underground Railroad or the route the escaping slaves took. (2)

4. People began referring to Harriett as Moses because she led her people out of slavery (2). In fact, she led more than 300 slaves to freedom (1).

5. Harriett worked as a spy (1) and a nurse (1) during the Civil War. She opened a home for sick, poor, and homeless blacks (2), and she worked to make it possible for women to vote (1).

Passage #7: George Washington Carver

1. George Washington Carver was orphaned as an infant (1). To find a school that would accept blacks, he had to leave his adoptive parents' home at the age of 12 (1).

2. At the age of 12 he left his home to find a school that would accept blacks (2). He travelled through three states (1). He had to work all along the way by doing laundry, cooking, and farm work (1).

3. George Washington Carver found hundreds of uses for peanuts, cowpeas, and sweet potatoes (all 3 = 2 pts.).

4. George Washington Carver received a degree in botany (1). He became director of Iowa State College's greenhouse (1). After he earned a Master's degree (1), he became a college professor (1) and chairman of the Agriculture Department (1) at Tuskegee Institute. The National Association for the Advancement of Colored People awarded George Washington Carver a medal for his achievement in agricultural chemistry (1). Two universities awarded him honorary doctorate degrees (1).

5. George Washington Carver assisted black farmers by going right into their fields to teach them how to grow better crops (2). He showed society that a black man could be a successful college professor (1) at a time when few blacks even attended college. He left scholarship money for black students who wanted to study chemistry, botany, or agriculture (2).

Passage #8: Clara Barton

1. Clara became involved in nursing for the first time when her brother was injured and she nursed him back to health (1). The Civil War was the time that Clara officially became the first American battlefield nurse (1). She also worked as a nurse during the Franco-Prussian war (1).

2. During her lifetime, Clara Barton was a public school teacher (1), a government clerk (1), a battlefield nurse (1), a public speaker (1), and president of the American Red Cross (1).

3. Clara had problems with laryngitis, which caused her to lose her voice when she was a teacher (1), so she took a job as a government clerk because it didn't require her to use her voice. Then when she was a speaker, she lost her voice again (1), so she had to leave that career, too.

4. Dansville, the town where Barton lived, had organized a Red Cross Chapter (1). This chapter responded immediately to a disaster in Michigan where forest fires had killed many people (1). The organization worked so well that the U.S. government decided to create the American Red Cross (1).

5. The American Red Cross is a branch of the International Red Cross (1). The U.S. president signed it into law in March of 1882 (1). That July, Clara Barton became the first president of the American Red Cross (1). Like the International Red Cross, during wartime the American Red Cross makes sure that injured soldiers get immediate medical care (1). Any hospital with a Red Cross flag is not supposed to be attacked (1), and Red Cross personnel will help anyone in need (1). The American Red Cross also offers help during peacetime disasters (1).

Famous Persons (cont.)

Answer Key (cont.)

Passage #9: Leonardo da Vinci

1. Leonardo was born in Italy (1) in 1452 (1), but his father refused to marry his mother because she was poor (1).

2. He studied the animal kingdom (1) and became an apprentice to the famous sculptor, Verrocchio (1). He always tried to invent new things (2).

3. He stayed in touch with his birth mother throughout his life (1). He adopted a boy and continued to care for him even when he found out he was a thief (1). Later, he adopted another son (1).

4. Leonardo da Vinci wrote about all the details for his amazing inventions backwards. (2) He did this because he was a very private man (2) and didn't want it to be easy for others to read his notes (1).

5. Leonardo is remembered as having the greatest imagination in history (1). He painted two of the most widely recognized art pieces in the world (1). He left 10,000 notebook pages detailing numerous inventions (1). He planned and supervised the building of a castle in France (1). He designed Milan's system of canals and bridges (1).

Passage #10: Mother Teresa

1. Mother Teresa immediately requested to leave the convent where she worked (1). When she finally got permission, she left with nowhere to stay and almost no money (1). She lived on the streets with the homeless (1) helping them in any way she could (1).

2. Mother Teresa spent most of her life working with the ill and homeless in the slums (1) of Calcutta (1), a city in India (1).

3. When a homeless person was dying, she would carry them to a place where they could stay until they died (1). Mother Teresa would clean them (1) and give them medical care (1). She would give them the last rites of their religion, even if it differed from her own (1).

4. Although given the name Agnes at birth (1), when she became a nun, she took the name of Teresa (1). When she became the principal of a convent school, she earned the title of Mother (1).

5. At the time of her death, Mother Teresa had established a school (1), a home for lepers (1), an orphanage (1), a home for the dying (1), and two religious orders—the Missionary Sisters of Charity (1) and the Missionary Brothers of Charity (1).

Passage #11: John Barry

1. John Barry was a Catholic (1) and he hated how the British oppressed Catholics (1) in his homeland. He hoped to have more opportunities available to him in America (2).

2. John Barry was strict but kind to his crewmen (1). He required that they have no liquor aboard the ship (1), go to church on Sunday whenever possible (1), or listen to the Bible read aloud if they couldn't attend church (1).

3. John Barry helped change merchant ships into warships (1) and kept the British from blockading the Delaware River (1). He was the first to capture a British ship during the Revolutionary War (1) and fired the last shot at sea of the Revolutionary War (1).

4. There are four statues honoring John Barry (1). Two are in Philadelphia (1); Washington, D.C. has another (1); and there's also one where he was born (1) in Wexford, Ireland.

5. John Barry is considered the "Father of the American Navy" because he convinced the U.S. of the need for a standing navy (1). He helped establish the naval department (1) and was appointed captain of the first U.S. Navy (1). John Barry also helped get warships ready and served as a ship captain during the Revolutionary War (1).

Passage #12: Sandra Day O'Connor

1. Sandra Day O'Connor's parents owned an isolated cattle ranch, and during the 1930s—when Sandra Day O'Connor was a child—there was no chance for her to go to school there (1). Therefore, she went to live with her grandparents during the school year (1) to get a good education (1).

2. Sandra Day O'Connor had hoped to run her parents' cattle ranch (1), but when she went to law school (1), she decided to become a lawyer (1).

3. When she first graduated with a law degree, no one wanted Sandra Day O'Connor because she was a female (1), yet today she holds one of the most powerful judicial positions in America (1). Her career shows that opportunities for American women used to be very limited (1) but that women now have the chance for important, powerful jobs (1).

4. Sandra Day O'Connor was the first female in American history to become a majority leader for a state legislature (1), and she was also the first woman to be named a United States Supreme Court Justice (1).

5. As a United States Supreme Court Justice Sandra Day O'Connor listens to about 150 cases a year (1). The year runs from October to June (1). She decides what she thinks about each case (1). Sometimes she is one of the judges who agrees to make a ruling (1). Then she may write the majority opinion (1) Other times she disagrees with the ruling (1), and then she writes an opinion statement stating why she disagrees (1). Sandra Day O'Connor may choose to serve on the Supreme Court until she dies (1).

Newspaper Articles about Places
Outline Student Guide

What's Important about a Place?

1. Name of place: _____

2. Where is it in the world?_____

3. Weather/Temperature: _____

   _____

4. Physical Characteristics: _____

   _____

   _____

   _____

5. Unique Characteristics: _____

   _____

   _____

   _____

6. Types of plants & animals found there: _____

   _____

   _____

   _____

7. Interesting/Surprising Facts:_____

   _____

   _____

   _____

   _____

   _____

   _____

Newspaper Articles about Places (cont.)

Graphic Organizer

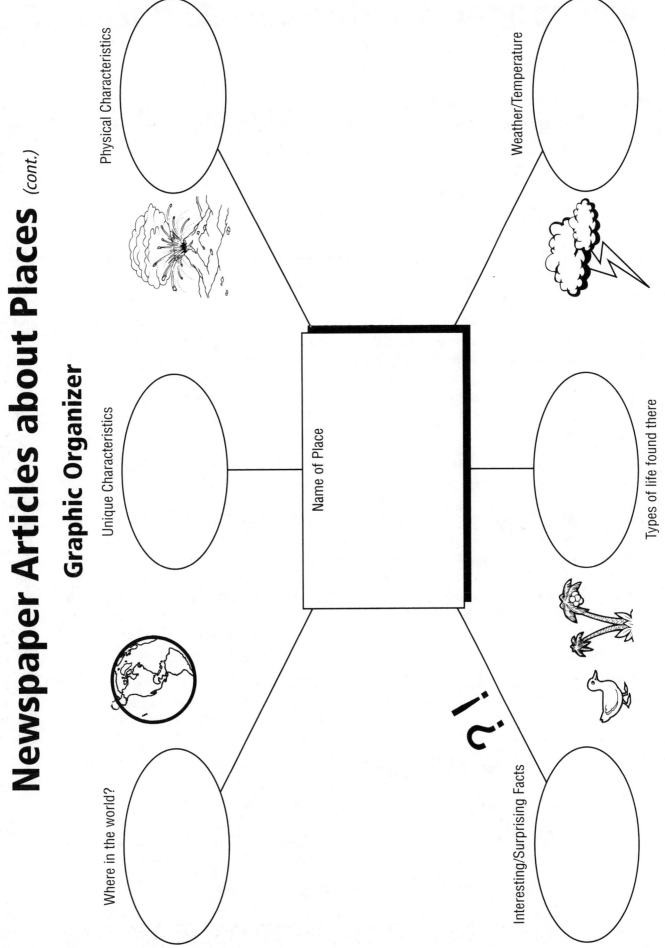

Physical Characteristics

Weather/Temperature

Unique Characteristics

Name of Place

Types of life found there

Where in the world?

Interesting/Surprising Facts

Newspaper Articles about Places (cont.)

Passage #1

Model the use of the outline on page 128 for this article.

Here are some words that you will need to know as you listen to this newspaper article:

coexist: live together
species: kinds
theorize: believe based on evidence
adapt: change

Six hundred miles west of Ecuador's shore lies a group of the most unusual islands in the world. Named the Galapagos Islands because of the gigantic tortoises that inhabit them, these 19 tiny land masses lie right on the equator and provide a home to some of the most unique plants and animals on Earth. Born from volcanoes deep beneath the ocean's surface, the islands have active volcanoes, spongy swamps, and forests of tangled bushes and vines. Unusual ocean currents result in four different oceanic environments. Cold water surrounds the islands while warm winds blow over the land, so animals that live in cold places and ones that live in warm ones coexist there. Penguins, once thought to only live in Antarctica, make their homes in the Galapagos in addition to the world's only marine iguanas.

Since the plants and animals on the Galapagos Islands share strong similarities to those found in South America, scientists theorize that during heavy rainstorms chunks of land large enough to hold several trees floated down South America's rivers and traveled out to sea, stopping when they collided with the islands. The plants and animals on these chunks of land developed in isolation, resulting in endemic species, which means species that live in only one place. In the 1800s while visiting the Galapagos Islands, Charles Darwin discovered the process of natural selection. Natural selection means that a plant or animal produces new features to adapt to its environment and increase its chances of survival. Those in each species most successful at adapting produce the most offspring and strengthen the species. Those that do not adapt die off. For example, the land iguanas had to learn to eat plants from the ocean floor or starve. Today, the Charles Darwin Research Station located on the largest island gives scientists the opportunity to conduct in-depth studies of the unique wildlife.

Since only one island has a year-round source of fresh water, very few people live on the islands. To prevent damage to the delicate environment, Ecuador has declared 96 percent of the Galapagos Islands a national park and limits the number of tourists to 40,000 annually.

Newspaper Articles about Places (cont.)

Passage #1 Questions

1. Tell about the features of the Galapagos Islands that make them so unique. (*7 points*)

_____

_____

_____

_____

_____

2. How do scientists explain why the plants and animals in the Galapagos Islands are so similar to those found in South America? (*3 points*)

_____

_____

_____

3. Explain how natural selection works and who discovered it. (*5 points*)

_____

_____

_____

_____

_____

4. Name three animals that live in the Galapagos Islands. (*3 points*)

_____

_____

5. Is anything being done to protect the Galapagos Islands? (*2 points*)

_____

_____

_____

Newspaper Articles about Places (cont.)

Passage #2

Use the outline on page 128 for this article.

Here are some words that you will need to know as you listen to this newspaper article:

erosion: the process of wearing away
petrified: wood changed into stone by minerals it has absorbed
plateaus: large, flat areas on the tops of hills or mountains

The state of Arizona has two of the seven natural wonders of the world. The first is the Grand Canyon—essentially a huge ditch created by the Colorado River's erosion of rock over a period of six million years. It extends across the state for 277 miles (446 km) and is about one mile (1.6 km) deep. In the years following the construction of the Glen Canyon Dam, the flow of the river and rate of erosion have lessened.

The second natural wonder is Meteor Crater (also known as Barringer Crater), a gigantic circular hole in the ground near Winslow. Scientists believe it formed when a meteorite struck Earth about 50,000 years ago, and they consider it the best crater of its kind in the world since it remains in almost perfect condition to this day. The crater measures 570 feet (175 m) deep by 4,180 feet (1,275 m) wide.

Although these two attractions are world-famous, they're certainly not Arizona's only fascinating features. The northeastern part of the state contains a 40-square mile (100 sq. km) petrified forest created 225 millions years ago when water seeped into coniferous logs. This water left behind mineral deposits which turned these logs into quartz and opal stones. Arizona also has the largest living ponderosa pine forest in the USA.

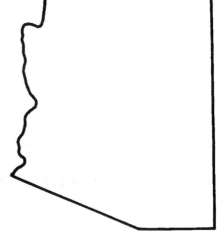

More than half the state consists of mountains and plateaus, yet the state also has a desert. In fact, its Painted Desert has earned a reputation for some of the most gorgeous sunrises and sunsets in the country. The Painted Desert, a brilliantly colored plateau region along the Little Colorado River, extends for 200 miles (320 km). The heat, light, and dust in this area makes the manganese and iron oxide in the rocks appear to change color. The blue, purple, and yellow colors visible at daybreak turn to rust, lilac, and blood red at sunset. The city of Tucson, nicknamed the "Astronomy Capital of the World," hosts 30 telescopes on nearby mountain peaks, including the largest solar telescope in the world. In 1930 the planet Pluto was discovered from the Lowell Observatory in Flagstaff, Arizona.

In 1912 Arizona joined the U.S. as the 48th state. Today, hundreds of thousands of tourists visit Arizona annually due to its stunning natural beauty and warm, dry winters. The state is also one of the nation's fastest growing areas; and during the last 50 years, Arizona's overall population has more than quadrupled.

Newspaper Articles about Places *(cont.)*
Passage #2 Questions

1. What are the areas of natural beauty found in Arizona? (*6 points*)

_____

_____

_____

_____

_____

2. Name and describe the two natural wonders of the world located in Arizona. (*5 points*)

_____

_____

_____

_____

_____

3. Choose one of Arizona's other fascinating natural features and tell how minerals helped to make it famous. (*2 points*)

_____

_____

_____

4. How did Tucson, Arizona, earn the title "Astronomy Capital of the World"? (*3 points*)

_____

_____

_____

5. Why do so many tourists visit Arizona each year? (*4 points*)

_____

_____

_____

Newspaper Articles about Places (cont.)

Passage #3

Model the use of the graphic organizer on page 129 for this article.

Here are some words that you will need to know as you listen to this newspaper article:

eroded: worn away
hibernation: spending a period of time in an inactive state
vegetation: plants
domesticated: trained to benefit people

The world's largest desert is the Sahara, covering one-seventh of our planet's land surface. It crosses 12 countries in North Africa. In the desert, almost all water is underground, but occasionally oases form, resulting in lush vegetation. Some areas are stony and mountainous, others flat and sandy. Sand dunes ranging in size from 3 to 1,200 feet (1–366 m) high and up to half a mile across blanket the Sahara. This sand consists of tiny grains of eroded rock. As sand gets blown about in a windstorm, it acts like sandpaper, wearing down other rock surfaces and allowing the desert to expand its territory. In fact, the Sahara Desert has expanded south for hundreds of years. Today, the Sahel, the semi-desert area at the southern fringe of the Sahara, has been overgrazed by farm animals, killing off necessary vegetation. As a result, the Sahel will probably become a part of the Sahara Desert.

Desert plants grow very slowly and live a long time by relying on extensive root systems. For example, grasses keep up to 85 percent of themselves underground. The visible portion of these plants can die until conditions are right for new growth to spring from their roots. To seek out water far underground, dwarf cypresses and acacia thorn bushes produce roots up to 250 feet (76 m) long.

The Sahara receives less than ten inches of precipitation annually. Desert air contains almost no water vapor, resulting in cloudless skies. During the day, the average air temperature reaches 105° F (41° C), and the ground temperature can reach 165° F (74° C). The hottest air temperature ever recorded on Earth was 136° F (58° C) in the Sahara. At night, temperatures often drop to the freezing point, which causes whatever water vapor is in the air to form dew. Some species rely on this for their water. To avoid the extreme temperatures of summer, many plants and animals have a summer hibernation called aestivation.

Desert animals include insects, scorpions, spiders, snakes, and lizards. The endangered addax and oryx antelope live there, too. All animals are scarce in the Sahara. As a result, a predator rarely encounters prey, and it must make a kill whenever it does. This causes desert snakes to produce powerful venom. Most desert animals spend their days hidden in deep burrows or under a piece of vegetation, emerging after sunset to hunt. Some predators never take a drink, relying solely on the body fluids of the food they capture to provide the liquid they need.

A well-known Sahara animal is the one-humped camel. Now totally domesticated, camels once lived wild in the desert. They store water in their stomachs and fat in their humps, allowing them to go for extended periods of time without food or water. With the discovery of salt mines and oil deposits in the Sahara, roads and airports have been built, so today camels transport tourists rather than commercial goods.

Newspaper Articles about Places (cont.)

Passage #3 Questions

1. What things mostly stay the same in the Sahara Desert? (5 points)

_____

_____

_____

_____

2. What things change in the Sahara Desert? (5 points)

_____

_____

_____

_____

3. What adaptations allow desert plants to survive the harsh conditions in the Sahara Desert? (4 points)

_____

_____

_____

_____

4. What are two different ways that animals in the Sahara Desert get the water they need to survive? (2 points)

_____

_____

_____

5. Tell four things you know about camels. (4 points)

_____

_____

_____

_____

Newspaper Articles about Places *(cont.)*

Passage #4

Use the graphic organizer on page 129 for this article.

Here are some words that you will need to know as you listen to this news article:

climate: typical weather conditions in a particular area over a long period of time
ecosystem: plants and animals sharing an environment
torrential: downpour

One of the world's most fascinating habitats, the Amazon tropical rainforest spreads over nine South American countries. It covers 2.3 million square miles (6 million square kilometers)—an area roughly the size of two-thirds of mainland America. Its climate has remained steady with plentiful warmth, rain, and sunshine for millions of years, remaining unaffected even during the Ice Age. Since it lies so near the equator, its high humidity and average temperature of 86° F (30° C) change very little from day to night or from month to month.

The Amazon has four different ecosystems, each with plants and animals adapting to the specific conditions of a rainforest layer. It starts with the forest floor, which has a blanket of rotting leaves. Here fungi and bacteria break down gigantic fallen trees and animal debris within days. Creatures such as poisonous frogs, giant anaconda snakes, panthers, and alligators live here. The understory, the area between the floor and 60 feet (18 m), has a constant humidity of 90 percent, with no wind and little sunlight. The next level, called the canopy, provides a home to the greatest number of plants and animals, including thousands of insects. Above it, the emergent layer must endure continuous sunshine and harsh winds. Here chattering monkeys, colorful parrots, and eagles make their homes. One mountainside in the Amazon contains a greater variety of plants than all those found in the United States! Yet even though at least half of the world's species of plants live here, the soil is acidic, and most of the fertility stays locked up in vegetation. As a result, the trees spread out bulging roots called buttresses to locate nutrients. Rootless plants grow on these trees' bark, getting nutrients from them.

The second largest river in the world, the Amazon, winds through the rainforest, giving a home to over 3,000 varieties of fish. The river begins as a trickle in the Andes Mountains and grows until its mouth is more than 100 miles (161 km) wide where it meets the Atlantic Ocean. The forest acts as a sponge, so despite the fact that the area receives 100 to 400 inches (254–1,016 cm) of rain annually, torrential rainstorm waters get released slowly into streams and rivers, reducing sudden, destructive floods.

Today, people threaten the Amazon, a tropical rainforest larger than all the other rainforests on Earth put together. Mining causes tremendous damage as people burn and bulldoze enormous areas to remove the soil in search of gold, copper, iron, and aluminum. Smelting also causes significant damage because many acres of trees must be cut to fuel the huge furnaces that heat the rocks to separate out the valuable metals. The logging industry has hacked roads through the forest to cut down the most desirable trees for furniture. The lack of these trees increases soil erosion, and the nutrients within these trees leave the forest forever. Dams built to provide hydroelectric power have backed up rivers, drowning every living thing within 1,500 square miles (3,885 square kilometers).

Scientists know that rainforests have a tremendous impact on the Earth's atmosphere and weather, and researchers have found more than 2,000 Amazon rainforest plants that have cancer-fighting chemicals. When people fully understand the importance of the rainforest, perhaps its destruction will stop.

Newspaper Articles about Places (cont.)

Passage #4 Questions

1. What is so unique about the temperature of the Amazon rainforest? (*3 points*)

   _____

   _____

   _____

2. Name the four different ecosystems that exist in the Amazon rainforest. (*4 points*)

   _____

   _____

   _____

   _____

   _____

3. Is the soil in the Amazon rainforest fertile? How do you know? (*4 points*)

   _____

   _____

   _____

   _____

4. Tell about the river that runs through the Amazon rainforest. (*5 points*)

   _____

   _____

   _____

   _____

5. How do people endanger the Amazon rainforest? (*4 points*)

   _____

   _____

   _____

   _____

Newspaper Articles about Places (cont.)
Passage #5

Do not use student guide pages for this article.

> Here are some words that you will need to know as you listen to this newspaper article:
>
> **hostile:** very unfriendly
> **trade winds:** the regular winds that help cause the circulation of the Earth's atmosphere

First seen in 1820 by sailors aboard both American and British vessels, Antarctica was the last continent discovered. As the fifth largest continent—as big as the USA and Mexico combined—it contains 10% of all the Earth's land mass, yet no one owns it. In 1841 a British expedition led by James Clark Ross discovered a gigantic floating ice cliff. Called the Ross Ice Shelf, it joins the Antarctic coast to the South Ocean and is 200 feet (61 m) high and over 600 miles (965 km) long.

Ross then journeyed far enough south to discover Mount Erebus, an active volcano, as well as the Transantarctic Mountains that divide the two enormous ice sheets that blanket the entire continent. These towering ice masses make Antarctica the highest continent on Earth. Since each is more than two miles thick, the ice sheets' weight has caused the majority of Antarctica's land mass to sink below the ocean's surface. The ice slowly moves about half a mile a year toward the edge of the continent. When it reaches the coast, huge chunks break off and float away as icebergs, some as large as two states combined.

Antarctica has a cold, bleak, hostile environment. Covered year-round almost entirely by ice, 90 percent of the sun's rays reflect off its surface, so little heat gets absorbed. As a result, the coldest temperature ever recorded on Earth occurred there in 1983. At -128° F (-89° C), it was colder than the surface of Mars. Antarctica is actually a desert since it receives so little precipitation each year. Its raging blizzards result from 200-mile-per-hour (322-kilometers-per-hour) winds whipping prior snowfalls across the barren landscape. The continent spends half of the year in darkness, for the sun disappears below the horizon in mid-March and doesn't reappear until mid-September.

In spite of these harsh conditions, Antarctica supports both plant and animal life. Its plant life includes lichens, bacteria, algae, and moss. Animals who make their home at least part of the year on Antarctica include insects, penguins, seals, birds, and ice fish. Antarctica even saw its first human birth in 1978 when an Argentine woman delivered her baby there. Although no one lives there permanently, 3,000 tourists travel to Antarctica annually.

Since 1956, Antarctica has served as a unique laboratory for scientists from around the globe. A 180,000-year-old ice core taken from an ice sheet supplies valuable historical scientific data. Air bubbles in the ice core show past volcanic eruptions and the changing levels of atmospheric gases. Due to its high elevation and dry air, Antarctica provides a home to three large telescopes positioned for astronomical observation. Scientists continue to study the nearly 10,000 meteorites that have fallen near the South Pole and seek to understand how Antarctica influences the Earth's trade winds and ocean currents.

Newspaper Articles about Places *(cont.)*

Passage #5 Questions

1. List the three major landmarks of Antarctica. (*3 points*)

_____

_____

_____

2. Do the enormous ice sheets that cover Antarctica ever move? What is the visible proof? (*3 points*)

_____

_____

_____

3. Has anyone ever been to Antarctica? (*4 points*)

_____

_____

_____

4. Why do people call Antarctica's environment hostile? (*4 points*)

_____

_____

_____

_____

5. Give a thorough explanation for why you agree or disagree with this statement:
   Nothing lives in Antarctica's harsh climate. *(6 points)*

_____

_____

_____

_____

_____

Newspaper Articles about Places (cont.)

Passage #6

Do not use student guide pages for this article.

Here are some words that you will need to know as you listen to this newspaper article:

ancestors: relatives (usually from long ago)
diverse: wide variety
photosynthesis: the process by which green plants change sunlight into food

As the largest coral reef on Earth, Australia's Great Barrier Reef is also the biggest structure created by living organisms and has been called one of the seven natural wonders of the world. Like most coral reefs, the Great Barrier Reef lies just under or slightly above the ocean's surface. Living coral forms the top layer, built upon the bodies of ancestors from thousands of years ago. Famous for its beauty, it extends for 1,250 miles (2,010 km) along the northeast coast of Australia at a distance that varies from 10 to 100 miles (16 to 161 km) from shore. Scientists believe that the Great Barrier Reef started forming about half a million years ago from the hardened skeletons of dead animals called coral polyps.

One of the world's most diverse ecosystems, many thousands of creatures live among the coral, ranging from microscopic, single-cell organisms to large mammals. About 1,500 species of fish and 200 kinds of birds call the reef home. Other inhabitants include crabs, giant clams, and sea turtles. Since the 1960s, newcomers called crown-of-thorns starfish have invaded the reef. Unfortunately, these creatures eat the living polyps, and no one knows how to stop them.

Billions of living polyps are attached to the reef, ranging in diameter from less than an inch (2.5 cm) to one foot (30 cm) across. Their colors include blue, green, purple, red, and yellow, giving the appearance of a gorgeous sea garden. Each coral is actually a tiny polyp with a limestone skeleton. Coral polyps live together in gigantic colonies. They attach themselves to each other with a flat sheet of tissue, then build up their limestone skeletons by removing calcium from the seawater and using it to deposit calcium carbonate around the lower half of their bodies.

Reef corals cannot survive without the single-cell algae that live in their own tissue. The polyps use the food created and released by this algae to create their limestone skeletons. As a result, coral reefs occur only in shallow, tropical waters that have enough sunlight to allow this algae to conduct photosynthesis.

Coral polyps reproduce in two ways. They produce eggs that hatch into tiny forms that swim away to start new colonies. They also reproduce by budding. Budding occurs when small, knob-like growths appear on the adult polyps' bodies. When these grow large enough, they detach from the parent and begin depositing their own limestone into the same colony.

In 1975 Australia formed the Great Barrier Reef Marine Park Authority, declared almost all of the reef a national park, and made it illegal to remove any coral. Each year, the reef attracts thousands of tourists, and petroleum companies want to drill in the area for oil. Scientists worry about possible damage to the reef from these interferences, but Australia has vowed to protect the reef since it is essential to the economic well-being of the fishing industry.

Newspaper Articles about Places (cont.)

Passage #6 Questions

1. Explain how tiny coral polyps created the Great Barrier Reef of Australia. (*5 points*)

_____

_____

_____

_____

2. Name six different animals that make their home at the Great Barrier Reef. (*6 points*)

_____

_____

_____

_____

3. Why do coral reefs only happen in shallow tropical waters? (*3 points*)

_____

_____

_____

4. Explain the two ways that coral polyps reproduce. (*3 points*)

_____

_____

_____

_____

5. Describe the things that threaten the Great Barrier Reef today. (*3 points*)

_____

_____

Newspaper Articles about Places (cont.)

Use this scoring guide in conjunction with the answer key to assess student performance.

Scoring Guide			
Points Possible	**Exemplary Score**	**Average Score**	**Minimum Passing Score**
20	18–20	15–17	12

Answer Key

Passage #1: Galapagos Islands

1. The Galapagos Islands are very unique because they have four different oceanic environments (1). Cold water surrounds the islands (1) but warm air is over the land (1). This allows animals that usually live in cold places and ones that usually live in warm places to live together there (1). These islands were created by volcanoes (1), and have spongy swamps (1) and forests of tangled bushes and vines (1).

2. Scientists believe that large chunks of land containing plants and animals floated out to sea from South American rivers (1), stopping when they collided with the islands (1). The animals and plants on these chunks of land lived in isolation, resulting in plants and animals that live only in one place (1).

3. Charles Darwin discovered the process of natural selection (1) when he visited the Galapagos Islands. Natural selection means that plants and animals (1) produce new features (1) to adapt to the environment (1) in a way that will increase their chances of survival (1).

4. Some animals that live in the Galapagos Islands include giant tortoises (1), marine iguanas (1), and penguins (1).

5. Almost all of the Galapagos Islands have been declared a national park (1) by Ecuador, and only 40,000 tourists are allowed to visit each year (1).

Passage #2: Arizona

1. Some areas of natural beauty in Arizona include the Grand Canyon (1), Meteor Crater (1), Petrified Forest (1), Painted Desert (1), the largest Ponderosa pine forest in the USA (1), and mountain and plateaus (1).

2. The Grand Canyon is a natural wonder of the world (1). It is a deep ditch (valley) with steep sides created by the Colorado River wearing away rock (1). Another natural wonder of the world is Meteor Crater (1). Meteor Crater was created when a meteorite struck Earth (1) tens of thousands of years ago. The Crater remains in almost perfect condition (1).

3. The Petrified Forest was formed when water seeped into logs and then left behind minerals (1) that turned the logs into quartz and opal rocks (1). **OR** Magnificent, different colors appear at sunrise and sunset in the Painted Desert due to the manganese (1) and iron oxide (1) contained in the rocks.

4. Tucson, Arizona, earned the title of "Astronomy Capital of the World" because there are 30 telescopes located nearby (1), and the planet Pluto was discovered by one of the telescopes (1). Tucson also has the largest solar telescope in the world (1).

5. So many tourists visit Arizona because of its natural beauty (1) and warm, dry winters (1). Others come because of their interest in astronomy (1) or to see some of the best sunrises and sunsets in America in the Painted Desert (1).

Passage #3: Sahara Desert

1. In the Sahara Desert the daytime temperature is always very hot (1) and the nighttime temperature is always cold (1), sometimes reaching the freezing point. There is always very little rainfall (1) and the types of plants (1) and animals (1) that live there don't really change.

2. The Sahara Desert's territory is always expanding (1). Shifting sand dunes change the landscape constantly (1). Sandstorms erode rock, increasing the amount of sand (1). Roads and airports have recently been built there (1). The camel no longer lives wild in the Sahara (1).

3. Many plants go through aestivation (summertime hibernation) to avoid the summer heat (1). The plants develop extensive root systems to seek out water (1). Many plants keep the majority of themselves under the ground (1) and only grow when the conditions are right (1).

4. Some animals get the water they need by drinking the dew that forms overnight (1). Others get the liquid they need from the fluids in the bodies of the animals they eat (1).

5. Since camels store water in their stomachs (1) and fat in their humps (1), they can go for a long time without food or water (1). There are no wild camels in the Sahara anymore (1). Today camels are used to transport tourists through the desert (1).
(Any 4 = 4 pts.)

Newspaper Articles about Places *(cont.)*

Answer Key *(cont.)*

Passage #4: Amazon Rain Forest

1. The day and night temperature remain about 86° F (30° C) in the Amazon rainforest (1), and the temperature does not vary much from month to month (1). In fact the temperature in the Amazon rainforest has been pretty much the same for millions of years (1), even during the Ice Age.

2. The four ecosystems that exist in the Amazon rainforest are: the forest floor (1), the understory (1), the canopy (1), and the emergent layer (1).

3. The soil is not fertile (1). It's actually acidic (1), and most of the nutrients stay locked up in the plants and trees (1). I know because to find the scarce nutrients, trees must spread out bulging roots (1) called buttresses.

4. The Amazon River flows through the Amazon rainforest (1). The Amazon River begins in the Andes Mountains (1) and empties into the Atlantic Ocean (1). It is the second largest river in the world (1), and it contains over 3,000 different kinds of fish (1).

5. People endanger the Amazon rainforest in four ways. Some burn or bulldoze large areas to mine for metals (1). Then they cut enormous numbers of trees to run furnaces that remove (smelt) the metal from the rocks and soil (1). Loggers cut down many of the most desirable trees (1) for furniture, and dams have drowned plants and animals for thousands of square miles (square kilometers) (1).

Passage #5: Antarctica

1. The three major landmarks of Antarctica are the volcano Mt. Erebus (1), the Ross Ice Shelf (1), and the Transantarctic Mountains (1).

2. Yes, Antarctica's ice sheets move slowly toward the edge of the continent (1). When the ice reaches the coast, big chunks break off and float away (1). These chunks are called icebergs (1).

3. Yes, a man named Ross explored the continent (1). Scientists operate a laboratory and telescopes there (1). A woman gave birth to a baby in Antarctica (1), and 3,000 tourists visit each year (1).

4. People call Antarctica's environment hostile because it is covered by ice year round (1) and spends half the year in darkness (1). The coldest temperature ever recorded on Earth happened in Antarctica (1), and it has blizzards with extremely high winds (1).

5. I disagree because Antarctica has both plants and animals living there (1). The plants include lichens, bacteria, algae, and moss (any 2 = *2 points*). The animals that make their homes there include insects, penguins, seals, birds, and fish (any 2 = *2 points*). Also, researchers live in Antarctica, although not permanently (1).

Passage #6: Great Barrier Reef

1. Tiny coral polyps created the Great Barrier Reef by taking calcium from the ocean water (1) and using it to make a limestone skeleton (1). These skeletons are left behind when the polyps die and a new layer of polyps build upon them (1). These living coral attach themselves to each other with a flat sheet of tissue (1). This process has gone on for millions of years (1), which is why the Great Barrier Reef is so large.

2. Animals that make their home at the Great Barrier Reef include coral polyps (1), fish (1), birds (1), crabs (1), giant clams (1), sea turtles (1), and crown-of-thorns starfish (1). (Any 6 = 6 pts.)

3. Shallow water allows enough sunlight to come through to let the algae do photosynthesis (1). This algae provides the food that lets the polyps create their limestone skeletons (1). Many layers of these skeletons build up, creating the coral reef (1).

4. One way that coral polyps reproduce is by eggs that hatch into tiny new polyps (1). Another way that coral polyps reproduce is by budding, which means that little growths appear on adults' bodies (1). When these growths get big enough, they detach from the parent (1).

5. Crown-of-thorns starfish eat the coral polyps (1). Disruption and pollution caused by the many tourists that visit the area can damage the reef (1). Petroleum companies want to drill for possible oil deposits in the area (1).

Newspaper Articles about Events
Outline Student Guide

What's Important about an Event?

1. When did it happen? _____
_____

2. Where did it happen? _____
_____

3. Why did it happen? (main causes) _____
_____
_____

4. Who were the major figures? _____
_____

5. What happened first? _____
_____
_____

6. What happened second? _____
_____
_____

7. What happened third? _____
_____
_____

8. What happened last? _____
_____
_____

9. What was the end result? _____
_____
_____

10. Were there any lasting effects? _____
_____

Newspaper Articles about Events *(cont.)*

Graphic Organizer

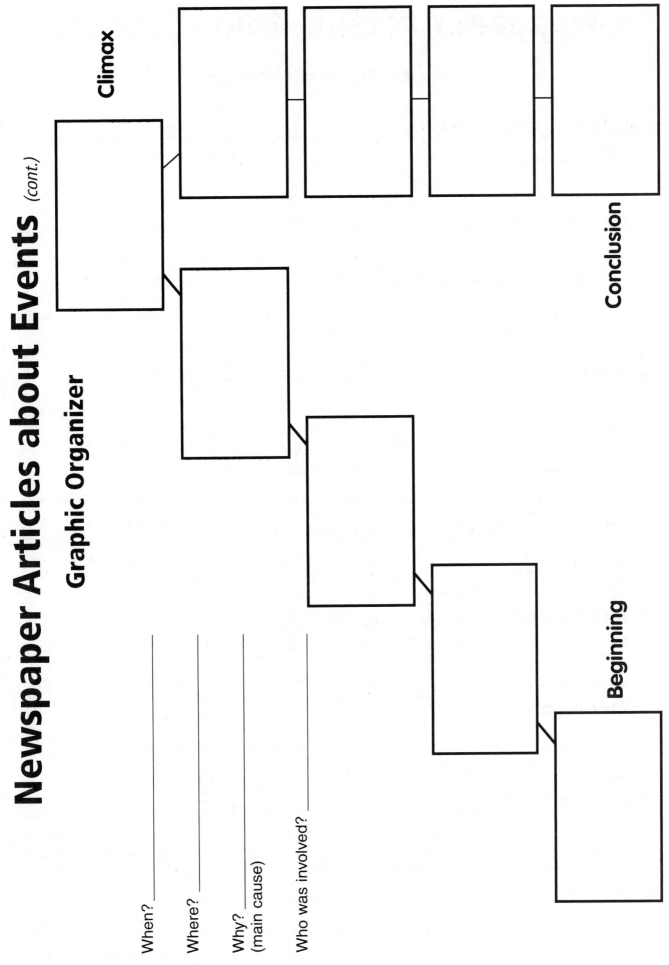

Climax

Conclusion

Beginning

When? _____

Where? _____

Why? _____
(main cause)

Who was involved? _____

Newspaper Articles about Events (cont.)

Passage #1

Model the use of the outline on page 144 for this article.

Here are some words that you will need to know as you listen to this newspaper article:

eliminate: get rid of
ambush: surprise attack

During World War II, the Japanese wanted to destroy all American ships. They had already destroyed much of the American fleet during a surprise attack on Pearl Harbor in Hawaii. Now the Japanese planned to eliminate the remaining ships with an ambush at Midway Island. However, the U.S. broke the code used for some of the Japanese radio messages and therefore knew many—although not all—of the details about the coming battle plan.

Since Midway Island lies about halfway between Japan and Hawaii, the Japanese knew the Americans would come to its rescue to prevent their enemy from establishing a base there. Such a base would allow the Japanese to more easily attack Hawaii and the West Coast of America.

The Japanese commander, Admiral Yamamoto, had four aircraft carriers in the Pacific Ocean, while the American commander, Admiral Nimitz, had only three. Aircraft carriers were the largest and most important ships because airplanes could take off and land on them.

At 4:30 a.m. on June 4, 1942, the Japanese launched the planes from their aircraft carriers to attack Midway Island. They hoped to lure all the U.S. aircraft carriers to the area in defense of the island. The U.S. had already sent up scout planes to find the Japanese fleet but these planes couldn't locate the Japanese aircraft carriers until 5:30 a.m. The Americans immediately sent many torpedo planes, each armed with a single torpedo, as well as bombers. The bombers could dive towards enemy ships and release their bombs only if they got close enough.

At 6:30 a.m., the Japanese attacked Midway Island. Within half an hour the Japanese planes had dropped all their bombs and started their long flight back to their carriers. Meanwhile the U.S. torpedo bombers were battling with the Japanese aircraft carriers, which had anti-aircraft guns and a group of fighter planes for defense. During the next three hours, the Japanese shot down more than 30 of the American torpedo planes and almost 70 American bombers.

A Japanese victory appeared certain, but then additional American bombers came out of the cloud cover and attacked. Within six minutes, three of the four Japanese aircraft carriers were almost completely destroyed. From their only remaining aircraft carrier, the Japanese launched a counterattack, but the U.S. fended them off, losing one aircraft carrier in the battle.

Later, the U.S. scout planes discovered the location of the last remaining Japanese aircraft carrier. The Americans attacked and mortally wounded it. The Japanese retreated. For two more days, the Americans pursued them, causing additional damage. This resulted in the first Japanese defeat in the Pacific.

The Battle of Midway is remembered because it turned the tide of the war in the Pacific in America's favor.

146

Newspaper Articles about Events *(cont.)*

Passage #1 Questions

1. What were the Japanese hoping to accomplish at Midway Island? (*3 points*)

_____

_____

_____

2. Why were the Americans so determined to keep the Japanese from taking control of Midway Island? (*2 points*)

_____

_____

_____

3. List the five kinds of military vehicles that participated in the Battle of Midway. (*5 points*)

_____

_____

_____

4. Outline the eight major events in the Battle of Midway in the order in which they occurred. (*8 points*)

_____

_____

_____

_____

_____

_____

_____

5. Is the Battle of Midway regarded as significant? Why or why not? (*2 points*)

_____

_____

_____

Newspaper Articles about Events *(cont.)*

Passage #2

Use the outline on page 144 for this article.

> Here is a word you will need to know as you listen to this news article:
>
> **habitats:** environments in which particular creatures live

Prior to 1988, Yellowstone National Park's last huge forest fire occurred during the 1700s. Yet the forest actually needs fire; otherwise, too many nutrients get locked up in dead and living trees. Fire encourages greater plant and animal variety by creating new habitats; in fact, the largest number of species occurs about 25 years afterwards. Fires also prevent forests from taking over the meadows where animals such as elk feed. After a large fire, these meadows grow vigorously, nourished by the nutrients released by the blaze. When scientists discovered these benefits in 1972, a new national park policy went into effect stating that if a fire started as the result of a lightning strike, no one would fight it unless it threatened private property or the park buildings. Most fires caused by lightning usually go out by themselves within hours, so this would result in minimal damages while allowing natural and necessary blazes.

However, in 1988 Yellowstone officials had to abandon their policy. During the summer of 1988—the driest summer in over 100 years—June had only a fraction of its average rainfall, and July had absolutely none. Many of the Park's old lodgepole pines had died and fallen to the ground during windstorms. Due to the dry climate, these dead trees didn't decay and covered the forest floor like logs in a fireplace.

On June 14 lightning started a fire that was left to burn. However, it didn't go out naturally, and after a month went by, things looked grim. Eight thousand acres (3,238 hectares) had already burned and high winds coupled with no rain encouraged several separate fires to grow dangerously fast. Finally, on July 21 officials decided to fight the fires. Two days later they realized that the fires were burning totally out of control.

Firefighters created firebreaks by bulldozing trees in front of an advancing fire to keep it from crossing the area. Overhead, planes dropped chemicals, and helicopters dumped water on the flames. In desperation, the workers deliberately burned areas to destroy fuel for the fire. However, the wind carried flaming bits of material which started still more fires. Even worse, some of these blazes started behind firefighters, trapping them between two advancing fires. More than a quarter of a million acres (101,174 hectares) had burned by August 20, the day called Black Saturday. Eighty-mile-per-hour (129 kph) winds spread all the separate fires, moving some as fast as three miles per hour (5 kph). That day, the thick smoke made the noon sky as dark as sunset.

Although 9,500 firefighters could not get the fire under control, the snow that fell in September did. Some areas still smoldered until November. Eight gigantic blazes had ravaged almost half of the Park, consuming just under a million acres (405,000 hectares). Officials decided to fight all future fires in national parks and forests.

Yellowstone's forest showed new growth just one year after the fire. Since lodgepole pines produce cones that actually require the high temperatures created by fire to open and deposit their seeds, tiny saplings poked up through the charred ground. A flowering plant called fireweed blanketed the area.

After about 200 years, Yellowstone will burn again and the cycle will start over.

Newspaper Articles about Events (cont.)

Passage #2 Questions

1. Explain why the National Parks had adopted a new policy in 1972 toward forest fires caused by lightning strikes. (*7 points*)

_____

_____

_____

_____

_____

2. Tell about the different methods used to try to stop the forest fires raging through Yellowstone National Park. (*4 points*)

_____

_____

_____

_____

3. What happened on Black Saturday? (*3 points*)

_____

_____

_____

4. What caused the fires to finally stop burning out of control? How much time passed between the start of the forest fire and when the blazes were finally under control? (*4 points*)

_____

_____

5. Explain why you agree or disagree with the following statement:

   One year after the huge fire at Yellowstone National Park, signs of new life were seen. (*2 points*)

_____

_____

_____

_____

Newspaper Articles about Events *(cont.)*

Passage #3

Model the use of the graphic organizer on page 145 for this article.

Here are some words that you will need to know as you listen to this newspaper article:

migration: large numbers of people moving from one area to another
drought: long period without any rain
enacted: passed a law
region: area

John Steinbeck, a famous American author, wrote a novel called *The Grapes of Wrath* about an actual event in American history—the migration of farm families from the Midwest to California during the 1930s. After years of record-breaking drought had scorched their land, these families abandoned what had once been profitable farms in the hopes of a better life on the West Coast.

Part of what caused this crisis was the fault of Nature and part was caused by human ignorance. Although the first Midwestern farmers had struggled to plow just two acres (one hectare), by the 1920s farmers had adopted modern farm equipment which allowed them to easily plow 50 acres (20 hectares). The farmers were proud of their many acres with long, straight rows of crops and pleased that none of their land was taken up by trees. Unfortunately, these two factors, along with the extended drought, led to large clouds of dirt being blown into the air, causing the once-fertile soil to actually blow away.

In 1932, 14 of these dust storms severely damaged the region, and the next year 38 more occurred, prompting a reporter from the *Washington Evening Star* to refer to the affected area as "the Dust Bowl." The Dust Bowl included Oklahoma and parts of Texas, Kansas, Colorado, and New Mexico.

Many exceptionally good growing years and record-breaking crop yields had occurred during the 1920s. All that changed when a drought started in 1931 and lasted until 1937. In fact, between 1933 and 1936, 20 plains states set records for lack of rain. Without rain, the crops began to shrivel up in the fields. Then swarms of grasshoppers attacked the crops. Adding to the farmers' troubles, thousands of hungry rabbits came down from the hills to eat the surviving crops. To make matters worse, the Great Depression caused crop prices to fall drastically, making the few crops that could be harvested worth very little. This left many farmers penniless, forcing banks to take over ownership of many farms and leaving the businesses that relied on the farmers, such as hardware and clothing stores, without customers.

However, the final straw was the terrible dust storms with winds that reached up to 70 miles per hour (113 kph) and carried away millions of tons of dirt as far east as Washington, D.C. The dust suffocated livestock and blew into tiny cracks in the Midwestern homes. Sometimes so much dust collected in the attics that it caused the ceilings in the houses to collapse. Many people died from dust pneumonia. Year after year of these relentless dust storms resulted in half a million people leaving to seek jobs as common laborers in California.

The federal government gradually enacted plans to help those who stayed. The United States Department of Agriculture helped the farmers to use such techniques as planting trees between the fields as a windbreak, rotating crops, and planting crops in rows running across the typical wind pattern.

Newspaper Articles about Events (cont.)

Passage #3 Questions

1. Explain the factors that led up to the creation of the Dust Bowl. (*4 points*)

_____

_____

_____

_____

2. What happened to many farm families living in the Dust Bowl? (*5 points*)

_____

_____

_____

_____

3. Name four of the five states affected by the Dust Bowl. (*4 points*)

_____

_____

_____

4. In addition to the awful dust storms, the farmers in the area had many other problems growing and selling their crops. What were these problems? (*4 points*)

_____

_____

_____

_____

5. Describe the three methods used today to prevent further Dust Bowl situations from happening. (*3 points*)

_____

_____

_____

_____

Newspaper Articles about Events *(cont.)*

Passage #4

Use the graphic organizer on page 145 for this article.

> Here are some words you will need to know as you listen to this newspaper article:
>
> **inhabitants:** residents
> **tsunami:** gigantic tidal wave

During May of 1883 the volcano on Krakatoa—a tiny island in the Indian Ocean—began spewing ash and smoke. Over the next three months the volcano occasionally grumbled and trembled, but because it hadn't erupted for more than 200 years, no one could have anticipated the disaster that occurred on August 27, 1883.

Formed over millions of years from lava flowing up from the ocean floor, Krakatoa was one of several volcanoes in the area. It towered 2,700 feet (823 m) above sea level. Although nobody lived on Krakatoa, thousands of people made their homes 40 miles (64 km) away on the Indonesian islands of Sumatra and Java. Many moved to higher ground when they first felt the earth tremors and saw the volcanic dust and large clouds of smoke and steam, but eventually they had to return to their farms and homes near the shore.

At 5:30 A.M. on that fateful August morning, Krakatoa erupted so violently that it awoke people thousands of miles away in Australia. Another explosion occurred a little over an hour later, but Krakatoa wasn't finished yet. Shortly after 10 A.M., the island blew up with more force than 1,000 atom bombs. Two-thirds of the island shot into the air, forming a gigantic cloud 50 miles (80 km) high. Inhabitants of Rodrigues Island 4,776 miles (7,686 km) to the southwest actually heard this tremendous blast. This eruption removed so much of the center of the island that the remaining land collapsed into the now empty center, causing another incredible blast just before noon. At that point, so much of the island had disintegrated or collapsed that the sea water poured in to fill the new 1,000-foot-deep (305 m) crater. This water collided in the center, then rushed back out as a 100-foot-high (31 m) tsunami racing at a speed of 350 miles per hour (563 kph) toward Java and Sumatra. These islands suffered a terrible blow when the tsunami hit. It wiped out hundreds of their villages, and 36,000 people died.

Some of the only surviving eyewitnesses were less than 30 miles (48 km) out to sea on a ship named *The Charles Bal.* When the captain saw lightning bolts in the boiling clouds of ash and steam, he ordered everyone to go below deck, then took down the sails to prevent them from being ripped to shreds by the hurricane-force winds carrying volcanic dust. Although buried under a thick cement-like layer of ash and mud, the ship and its terrified occupants lived to tell their tale to an astonished world.

Afterwards, magnificent sunsets in unusual red, pink, and purple hues occurred all over the world. Lava continued to flow from deep within the Earth, causing a new island to appear in 1925 in the place where Krakatoa once stood. People named it Anak Krakatoa, which means child of Krakatoa. So far, it has reached a height of 300 feet (90 meters), and it continues to grow even today.

Newspaper Articles about Events (cont.)

Passage #4 Questions

1. Where was Krakatoa located? Was there any land nearby? (*4 points*)

_____

_____

_____

2. Describe what the people on the *Charles Bal* experienced when Krakatoa blew.
   (*5 points*)

_____

_____

_____

_____

3. Explain what a tsunami is and how it is formed. (*4 points*)

_____

_____

_____

_____

4. Explain why you agree or disagree with this statement:

   The worst part of Karakatoa's eruptions was all the damage caused by the lava flows.
   (*4 points*)

_____

_____

_____

_____

5. What does the site where Krakatoa once stood look like today? (*3 points*)

_____

_____

_____

Newspaper Articles about Events *(cont.)*

Passage #5

Do not use the student guide pages for this article.

Here are some words you will need to know as you listen to this newspaper article:

sparsely: very little
antimatter: matter which has particles that are the opposite of the particles in matter

Shortly after 7 A.M. on June 30, 1908, the biggest explosion ever recorded on Earth occurred near Tunguska, Siberia, in a remote and sparsely populated part of Russia. To this day, no one has ever figured out exactly what happened, but everyone agrees that had it occurred most anywhere else in the world, the destruction and loss of human life would have been tremendous.

The power of the explosion was truly awesome, for it knocked people and large farm animals right off their feet more than 400 miles (644 km) from the center of the blast. It destroyed everything within a 24-mile (39-km) radius, leaving the landscape barren, blackened, and burned. Absolutely nothing remained standing. In fact, for 20 miles (32 km) trees lay flattened on the ground around a center point just like spokes on a bicycle wheel.

Eyewitnesses said they saw an object fall from the sky a few seconds before the blast caused such an intense brightness that it made the sun look dark in comparison. During the two months following the blast, highly unusual sunsets of green and bright yellow occurred frequently all over the continent of Europe. The nights never truly darkened, and people could read a newspaper outdoors at midnight.

Ever since that day, scientists have come up with a number of different theories as to what happened but cannot prove any of them. Due to the extremely high radiation levels measured at the site for years afterwards, most believe it was some sort of atomic explosion. Yet it occurred 36 years prior to the creation of the atom bomb, and was much more destructive than the first atomic bomb dropped at the end of the second World War. Since tiny crystals common to both asteroids and comets have been found at the site, one theory states that a comet or an asteroid collided with the Earth's atmosphere, causing a natural atomic explosion.

Some scientists claim that a meteorite composed of antimatter hit our planet. Everything on Earth consists of matter. When antimatter and matter touch, an intense explosion results. Researchers estimate that the object weighed 10,000 tons, so some people believe that a black hole hit the planet and was so heavy it fell right through, exiting someplace in the Atlantic Ocean.

In reality, we will probably never know with any certainty what occurred so long ago in Siberia.

Newspaper Articles about Events (cont.)

Passage #5 Questions

1. What happened at the time of the blast near Tunguska, Siberia? (*4 points*)

_____

_____

_____

2. What happened as a result of this blast? (*6 points*)

_____

_____

_____

_____

3. Discuss the theories scientists have come up with to explain this mysterious explosion. (*4 points*)

_____

_____

_____

_____

4. Why was it fortunate that the explosion occurred where it did? (*3 points*)

_____

_____

_____

5. Give three reasons why most people do not believe the explosion was caused by an atomic bomb. (*3 points*)

_____

_____

_____

_____

Newspaper Articles about Events *(cont.)*

Passage #6

Do the not use the student guide pages for this article.

> Here are some words you will need to know as you listen to this news article:
>
> **occupied:** took control of and stayed in
> **regions:** areas

After World War II, the U.S.S.R. occupied the eastern portion of the city of Berlin, the former Nazi capital of Germany. Other Allied Powers—including America, Britain, and France—occupied other parts of Berlin. On June 23, 1948 the Soviets suddenly announced that technical difficulties had halted all traffic into and out of East Berlin. The other Allies knew something was wrong, but didn't want to challenge the U.S.S.R. Instead, they organized hundreds of flights of supplies into East Berlin to prevent its people from starvation.

Later, when the other Allied powers withdrew from Berlin, Soviet forces remained in East Berlin, which they renamed East Germany. Again, fearing a conflict with the communist Soviet Union, the democratic Allied nations did not protest. Then, without warning, on August 13, 1961, East Germany's communist police and soldiers closed all of the border crossing points between East and West Germany, cut all telephone lines, and stopped postal services. The very next day work began on the Berlin Wall—a 20-foot high cement block structure topped with barbed wire. To make certain that no one could cross the border, 250 watch towers were added and 14,000 soldiers and dogs patrolled the Wall around the clock. The people to the west of the Wall called the Berlin Wall the "Iron Curtain," and its creation brought about the tension between the United States and the U.S.S.R called The Cold War. Over the next two decades, almost 600 East Germans died trying to escape over the Berlin Wall.

About 25 years later, Soviet Russia realized that it could no longer maintain its military presence throughout Europe while its citizens starved in the streets. In 1986 it began withdrawing its military forces from many regions. When Hungary destroyed its barbed wire barrier with Austria in May 1989, more than 150,000 East German citizens illegally escaped. Meanwhile, 1.8 million others, most of them the best-educated and well-trained people in East Germany, had applied to leave the country. The Soviet leader, Premier Mikhail Gorbachev, announced that he would not provide additional military support to prevent the East Germans from escaping to Hungary. More and more people fled, for once they made it to West Germany, they would receive a passport, cash, and low-interest loans from the West German government.

Just 32 days after Gorbachev had visited East Germany, the acting East German government announced that as of midnight November 9, 1989, East Germans would be free to cross the border for the first time in 28 years. At the stroke of midnight, a noisy, excited crowd gathered to take part in destroying the Wall. As they smashed chunks of concrete, they shouted, sang, danced, sprayed champagne, and blew horns. The noisy celebration marking the end of Communist rule in East Germany lasted for two whole days.

Newspaper Articles about Events *(cont.)*

Passage #6 Questions

1. How did the Soviets come to be in East Berlin in the late 1940s? (*1 point*)

   _____

   _____

2. More than a dozen years before the Berlin Wall was actually built, the U.S.S.R. had tried to seal the East German border. What did the Allies do in response? Why? (*3 points*)

   _____

   _____

   _____

   _____

3. Describe the methods that were used to make certain that no one could make it across the Berlin Wall. (*4 points*)

   _____

   _____

   _____

4. Why did the East Germans risk the dangers of trying to cross the Berlin Wall in order to get to West Germany? (*5 points*)

   _____

   _____

   _____

   _____

5. Tell everything that happened at the Berlin Wall when the East German government announced that its citizens were going to be allowed to cross the border. (*7 points*)

   _____

   _____

   _____

   _____

   _____

   _____

Newspaper Articles about Events (cont.)

Use this scoring guide in conjunction with the answer key to asses student performance.

Scoring Guide			
Points Possible	Exemplary Score	Average Score	Minimum Passing Score
20	18–20	15–17	12

Answer Key

Passage #1: Battle of Midway

1. The Japanese wanted to lure all the U.S. aircraft carriers into the area (1) to come to Midway Island's defense (1). Once there, the Japanese planned to destroy all of the American aircraft carriers (1).

2. The Americans didn't want the Japanese to take control of Midway Island because they didn't want them to establish a base there (1). If the Japanese had a base at Midway, it would be easier for them to attack Hawaii and the West Coast (1).

3. The five kinds of military vehicles that fought in the Battle of Midway were aircraft carriers (1), scout planes (1), fighter planes (1), torpedo planes (1), and bombers (1).

4. First, the U.S. found out some of the Japanese battle plan in advance (1). Second, the Japanese used bombers to attack Midway Island (1). Meanwhile, the U.S. planes attacked the Japanese aircraft carriers (1). The Japanese shot down many of these U.S. planes (1). Suddenly, more U.S. bombers appeared and attacked the aircraft carriers (1). Immediately, three of the four Japanese aircraft carriers were almost completely destroyed (1). The Japanese retreated (1). The U.S. chased the one remaining Japanese aircraft carrier and severely damaged it (1).

5. Yes, the Battle of Midway is regarded as important because it turned the war in the Pacific in the United States' favor (1). It was also the first Japanese defeat in the war in the Pacific (1).

Passage #2: Yellowstone Forest Fire

1. Scientists had discovered that forest fires are beneficial (1). Fires help plant and animal variety (1), create new habitats (1), keep the forests from overtaking the meadows (1), and help meadows grow better afterwards (1). Since fires begun by lightning strikes almost always went out by themselves (1), the new policy would allow natural and necessary blazes (1).

2. To eliminate the blaze's fuel, firefighters created firebreaks by bulldozing large areas (1) and setting small fires (1). Overhead planes dropped smothering chemicals (1), and helicopters dropped water (1).

3. On Black Saturday, 80-mile-per-hour winds caused the fires to spread (1) very rapidly (1). There was so much smoke in the sky that the noonday sun looked as dark as sunset (1).

4. The fires came under control when snow fell (1). The first fire started in mid June (6/14) (1), and the fires were under control by September (1), so about three months passed (1).

5. I agree with this statement because after one year lodgepole pine saplings (1) and fireweed (1) were seen growing in the burnt areas.

Passage #3: Dust Bowl

1. There was an extended drought in the area (1). Farmers there were farming more land than ever before (1). Since farmers had gotten rid of all the trees (1) and planted their crops in long, straight rows (1), the dry soil just blew away.

2. Many families lost their farms to the banks (1) because they had no money (1). Others had their ceilings collapse from all the dust in the attics (1). A lot of people got dust pneumonia (1). Some moved to California in hopes of getting jobs there (1).

3. The states involved in the Dust Bowl were Oklahoma (1), Texas (1), Kansas (1), Colorado (1), and New Mexico (1).

4. The crops shriveled up in the fields due to lack of rain (1). Grasshoppers attacked the crops (1). Thousands of rabbits ate the remaining crops (1). The Great Depression had caused crop prices to fall very low (1).

5. Farmers plant their crops in rows that go against the typical wind pattern (1), and they have added trees and bushes between fields (1). In addition, many farmers use crop rotation (1).

Answer Key *(cont.)*

Passage #4: Krakatoa's 1883 Eruption

1. Krakatoa was a tiny island in the Indian Ocean (1). Nearby there were two islands (1) named Java (1) and Sumatra (1).

2. The people on the *Charles Bal* saw lightning bolts (1) in the boiling clouds of ash and steam (1), and hid from hurricane-force winds (1) full of volcanic dust (1). Although their ship was buried under a thick layer of ash and mud (1), they lived through the disaster.

3. A tsunami is a gigantic tidal wave (1). It formed when Krakatoa blew up and sea water rushed into the hole where the volcano had been (1). This water smashed together in the middle (1), then rushed back out at an incredible speed (1).

4. I disagree (1). Actually the worst part of Krakatoa's eruptions was the huge tsunami (tidal wave) it caused. (1) The tsunami washed away many villages (1) and killed tens of thousands of people (1) on Java and Sumatra.

5. A new island named Anak Krakatoa stands where Krakatoa once stood (1). Lava flows continue to build this island up (1). So far, it has reached a height of 300 feet (90 meters) (1).

Passage #5: Mysterious Siberian Explosion

1. There was an intense brightness (1), and everything within a huge area was destroyed (1). People and large farm animals were knocked off their feet hundreds of miles away (1), and all the trees were flattened in a gigantic circle (1).

2. The landscape was left blackened and burned (1). All over Europe there were strange-colored sunsets (1) of green and bright yellow (1). The nights never truly got dark for months afterwards (1), and high levels of radioactivity remained in the area for years (1). Scientists have tried to explain what happened to cause all of these phenomena (1).

3. Many people think this mysterious explosion was caused when a comet or asteroid hit the Earth's atmosphere (1). Other scientists believe the cause was a meteorite made up of antimatter that struck the planet (1). Still others think that a black hole hit the Earth and was so heavy that it fell right through (1). Almost everyone agrees it was some kind of atomic explosion (1).

4. It's a good thing that the explosion occurred where it did because if a blast with that much force had happened almost anywhere else in the world, it would have caused much more destruction (1) and killed many people (2).

5. Most people don't believe the blast was caused by an atomic bomb because this explosion happened 36 years before the invention of the first atomic bomb (1) and was significantly more powerful than the first atomic bomb (1). In addition, no one had anything to gain by dropping a bomb in such a remote, unpopulated area (1).

Passage #6: Berlin Wall

1. After World War II, the Soviet military took control of and lived in East Berlin (1), the former capital of Germany.

2. The Allied nations did not want to challenge the U.S.S.R. (1), so they flew hundreds of flights full of supplies across the border (1). They did this to prevent the East Germans from starvation (1).

3. A very high cement block wall was put up (1) and topped with barbed wire (1). The Berlin Wall also had watch towers (1) and soldiers and dogs that continuously patrolled it (1).

4. The East Germans wanted to escape from Communist rule (1). They may have had family or friends in West Germany (1). They also knew that once they got there, the West German government would give them a passport (1), money (1), and low-interest loans (1).

5. A crowd of people formed at the Wall to destroy it (1). As they tore down the Wall, they shouted (1), sang (1), danced (1), and sprayed champagne (1), and blew horns (1). This celebration lasted for two entire days (1).

Bibliography

Armstrong, William. *Sounder.* HarperCollins, 1989. (Newbery Medal Winner, 1970.)

Babbit, Natalie. *Tuck Everlasting.* Farrar, Straus, & Giroux, 1986. (International Board of Books for Young People Award Winner, 1978; Christopher Award, 1975.)

Bauer, Marion. *On My Honor.* Yearling Books, 1987. (Newbery Honor Winner, 1987.)

Blos, Joan. *A Gathering of Days: A New England Girl's Journal, 1830–1832.* Aladdin Paperback, 1990. (Newbery Medal Winner, 1980.)

Fleischman, Sid. *The Whipping Boy.* Troll Associates, 1989. (Newbery Medal Winner, 1987.)

George, Jean Craighead. *Julie of the Wolves.* HarperTrophy, 1974. (Newbery Honor Winner, 1973.)

Howe, James and Deborah. *Bunnicula.* Aladdin, 1996. (ALA Notable Book; Dorothy Canfield Fisher Award Winner, 1981.)

L'Engle, Madeleine. *A Wrinkle in Time.* Yearling Books, 1973. (Newbery Medal Winner, 1963.)

Mohr, Nicholasa. *Felita.* Puffin, 1999. (National Council on Social Studies Notable Trade Book, 1980; Child Study Children's Book Committee Book of the Year, 1980.)

Sachar, Louis. *Holes.* Yearling Books, 2000. (Newbery Medal Winner, 1999.)

Taylor, Mildred. *Roll of Thunder, Hear My Cry.* Puffin, 1997. (Newbery Medal Winner, 1977.)

Yep, Laurence. *Dragon's Gate.* HarperTrophy, 1995. (Newbery Honor, 1994.)

(**Note:** All publication dates are for the paperback versions of these books.)